Concise
Seashore
Wildlife
Guide

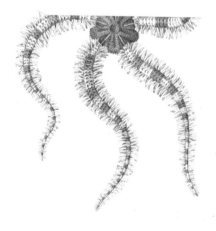

There are 47 individual Wildlife Trusts covering the whole of the UK and the Isle of Man and Alderney. Together The Wildlife Trusts are the largest UK voluntary organization dedicated to protecting wildlife and wild places everywhere – at land and sea. They are supported by 791,000 members, 150,000 of whom belong to their junior branch, Wildlife Watch. Every year The Wildlife Trusts work with thousands of schools, and their nature reserves and visitor centres receive millions of visitors.

The Wildlife Trusts work in partnership with hundreds of landowners and businesses in the UK. Building on their existing network of 2,250 nature reserves, The Wildlife Trusts' recovery plan for the UK's wildlife and fragmented habitats, known as A Living Landscape, is being achieved through restoring, recreating and reconnecting large areas of wildlife habitat.

The Wildlife Trusts also have a vision for the UK's seas and sea life – Living Seas, in which wildlife thrives from the depths of the oceans to the coastal shallows. In Living Seas, wildlife and habitats are recovering, the natural environment is adapting well to a changing climate, and people are inspired by marine wildlife and value the sea for the many ways in which it supports our quality of life. As well as protecting wildlife, these projects help to safeguard the ecosystems we depend on for services like clean air and water.

All 47 Wildlife Trusts are members of the Royal Society of Wildlife Trusts (Registered charity number 207238). To find your local Wildlife Trust visit wildlifetrusts.org

Concise
Seashore
Wildlife
Guide

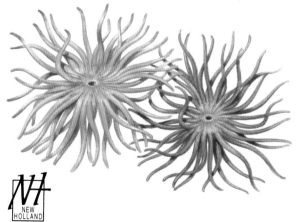

NH
NEW
HOLLAND

First published in 2011 by New Holland Publishers (UK) Ltd
London · Cape Town · Sydney · Auckland
www.newhollandpublishers.com
Garfield House, 86–88 Edgware Road, London W2 2EA, UK
80 McKenzie Street, Cape Town 8001, South Africa
Unit 1, 66 Gibbes Street, Chatswood, New South Wales 2067, Australia
218 Lake Road, Northcote, Auckland, New Zealand

10 9 8 7 6 5 4 3 2 1

ISBN 9 781 84773 786 1

Series Editor: Krystyna Mayer
Design: Alan Marshall
Artwork: Sandra Doyle, Bridgette James, Denys Ovenden, Melanie Perkins,
   Helen Senior and Lyn Wells
Production: Melanie Dowland
Publisher: Simon Papps

The publishers thank Lissa Goodwin of The Wildlife Trusts for reading the text.

Reproduction by Modern Age Repro Co. Ltd., Hong Kong
Printed and bound in China by Leo Paper Group

OTHER TITLES IN SERIES   *Concise Butterfly & Moth Guide*
                                Concise Bird Guide
                                Concise Wild Flower Guide
                                Concise Insect Guide
                                Concise Garden Wildlife Guide
                                Concise Tree Guide
                                Concise Mushroom Guide

Contents

Introduction

The *Concise Seashore Wildlife Guide* is a simple colour guide to 180 species of plant and animal that are likely to be seen mainly in the intertidal areas (also called the littoral zone) around the coasts of northern Europe. Many species occur within this narrow band where land meets the sea, so the book is selective. Mobile species such as birds have been given minimal coverage (pages 180–7), and rarities and species that are difficult to identify have been excluded. The selection represents a good range of species that are likely to be found and identified. A few terrestial plants that thrive on seashores just above the tide line are also included.

Characteristics of Seashore Wildlife

The seashore is unlike any terrestial habitat, and the plants and animals that occur on it are usually very different in form from their land-based relatives. Many of the straightforward structural and behavioural differences that allow plants to be distinguished from animals break down on the seashore. Plants are no longer just green, but all sorts of colours; there are animals that look like plants, and vice versa; and complex colonies of creatures of which the basic units are quite obscure to the casual observer. For this reason a whole habitat, rather than a single biological group like birds, insects, or flowers, is covered here. The species are laid out in taxonomic order within their groups, with related species together.

Zonation of Seashore Life

Because of the regular way in which tides move in and out, exposing different parts of the shore for different times, there is a clear zoning of seashore life according to how tolerant different species are of exposure to air and sunlight. The zonation is not always clearly visible, especially on sandy shores and irregular shores with variable changes in level. At other times, particularly on evenly sloped rocky shores, it can be very well marked, with clearly visible bands of differently coloured plants extending down to the shore. Because many species are quite precise in their requirements, a knowledge of this zonation can help in identification. It does not, of course, apply to washed-up or dislodged plants or animals, which can occur at any level.

Splash Zone

This is the highest zone. It is above the levels of the highest tides, but is strongly affected by salt spray, especially on exposed coasts, and the resident life is directly influenced by this. Black and orange lichens are particularly characteristic of this zone, together with salt-tolerant flowering plants such as Thrift, but no seaweeds normally occur here.

Upper Shore

This is the highest zone that is regularly inundated, although it is usually defined as the area above mean high water, but below the line reached by the highest spring tides, so it is not inundated by every high tide. It has relatively limited seashore life, but includes limpets, barnacles and other molluscs, as well as shore wracks and much strand-line debris. Although this zone is poor in species, what there is may occur in large numbers.

Middle Shore

The extensive area of shore between the average high-water level and the average low-water level is known as the middle shore. It is covered and uncovered by every tide, and makes up the bulk of what is thought of as the shore. Most of the typical seashore plants and animals occur here, often in great abundance, and there is a certain amount of zoning within this section, although it is not always visible.

Lower Shore

Below the average low-water level, there is a further area of shore that is accessible only at spring tide lows – that is, when the tide is unusually low. This is the lower shore. It is not accessible every day, but does support a fascinating range of wildlife, including many delicate species, such as sea urchins and anemones, which cannot withstand much exposure. It is the closest you can get to seeing true marine life without diving. There is also a submerged zone, which is home to bottom-dwelling animals such as lobsters, gobies, crabs and flounders.

Seashore Habitats

Seashores vary enormously in character, from exposed rocky coasts to sheltered estuaries or salt marshes. Each type of coast supports a different range of organisms, although the divisions between habitat types are not always clear cut, and some mobile or adaptable species may occur in more than one shore type. The main shore types that can be recognized are: rocky shores, sandy shores, shingle shores and muddy shores. These relate to the underlying geology of the coast, the degree of exposure of wave action, and the offshore current and sediments.

Rocky Shores

These can be divided into exposed and sheltered areas, although of course there is overlap between the two. Very large numbers of species occur, often in great abundance, on sheltered rocky shores. Relatively small changes in alignment can mean the difference between an area being sheltered or exposed, and the two types can often occur in close juxtaposition. They may often have sandy beaches in between, and thus present immense opportunities for finding species.

The rock type found on rocky shores has an important bearing on the fauna and flora found. Attached species are to some extent directly influenced by the chemical nature of the rock substrate, but more significant is the hardness of the rock and the way in which it weathers. A very fast-eroding rock supports relatively few species since they are constantly being sloughed off. A moderately soft rock may be very rich, allowing easy attachment and weathering into a wide variety of niches for creatures to fill. The amount of pools, cracks and indentations in the rock also has an important bearing on the life it supports.

Barnacles, limpets, urchins and chitons are probably the most common inhabitants of rocky shores, and kelp can be found at the water's edge.

Rock Pools

Although they are a feature of rocky shores, rock pools have a particular life of their own. The best pool-forming rock types are granite, some shales, hard limestones and basalt. Conditions within rock pools are unlike those on the open shore, since the life in them remains submerged whatever the state of the tide. However, they are subject to increased light, warming up, dilution of the salinity by rainwater and changes in the oxygen/carbon dioxide balance.

The higher up the shore a rock pool is, the more it is subject to these changes and, generally speaking, the less diverse the life it supports. The most interesting rock pools are thus well down the shore, not too exposed, deep enough and large enough to minimize fluctuations in temperature on very hot or very cold days, and preferably with additional dark crannies or overhanging areas. Such places are usually full of life.

Shallow pools may contain small beadlet anemones, seaweeds, small blennies and tiny crabs, with the rocky exposed sides being grazed on by limpets and periwinkles. Deeper pools are fringed by sturdier seaweeds, and may contain juveniles of fish species, large crabs and even lobsters.

Shingle Beaches

Unlike rocky shores, shingle beaches are the least diverse of intertidal environments. Shingle is composed of vast numbers of loose rounded stones, from pea sized to boulder sized, which are typically very mobile and unstable. In rough weather, shingle moves around considerably and smaller pebbles can easily be seen to move. It is the intense degree of mobility that prevents most forms of life from getting a foothold.

The middle and lower shores of a shingle beach are virtually devoid of life. Higher up, mobile invertebrates may scavenge in large numbers among detritus along the drift line. Above the high-water mark, a few flowering plants such as Sea Holly and Sea Beet can survive in this harsh environment.

Sandy Shores

Sandy beaches are the most familiar type of shore, but they are nothing like as rich in species as a sheltered rocky shore. Sand is made up of masses of tiny grains of varying size, shape and character, though always small enough to pack together tightly. They are mobile, like shingle, but often appear less so because they usually occur in flatter situations. They are also subject to severe wind movement when exposed for long.

The exposed surface of sand supports very little life. However, there is rather more life below the surface, some of which emerges to feed when the tide covers it. Oxygen and water are trapped in the tiny spaces between grains, allowing resident species to maintain a reasonably stable environment below the surface.

Typical sand beach residents include lugworms, various molluscs such as cockles and tellins, shrimps and some fishes.

Muddy Shores & Salt Marshes

In very sheltered situations where the force of the sea is minimal, such as estuaries and bays, the smallest suspended particles, including mud and silt, are deposited.

The sheltered nature of muddy situations allows many species to do well, particularly as such places may be very high in nutrients. Although the range of species is not generally large, the number and density of animals is often huge. Mudflats are one of the favoured feeding areas of vast numbers of waders and wildfowl in winter, because they are full of food and frost free. Where the force of wave action falls below a certain threshold and the land is not totally submerged, salt marsh may develop, colonized by various species of flowering plant such as Cord Grass, Sea Purslane and Marsh Samphire.

SEASHORE PLANTS

Seaweeds

The seaweeds, or algae, are a group of simple non-flowering plants that reproduce by spores. They are easily the most abundant of

Frond or blade

Midrib

TYPICAL BROWN SEAWEED
(e.g. TOOTHED WRACK)

Stalk or stipe

Holdfast

intertidal plants and exist in a huge variety of forms. Very few are green, because most have additional pigments to allow them to absorb light under water. All seaweeds have a simple structure, with no division into roots or leaves, though they may be highly divided into fronds or blades. They are normally attached to the substrate by a holdfast, and absorb all their food directly from sea water.

Seaweeds can be split into three groups according to their colour pigmentation – green, brown and red. **Green seaweeds** such as Sea Lettuce form only a minor part of most communities. The most obvious species are usually ***brown seaweeds***, which include the wracks and kelp, and often dominate much of the shore. ***Red seaweeds*** are less obvious but often abundant. They are usually small and not very conspicuous, and vary from types that look almost like red cabbages to encrusting types that look more like lichens.

Flowering Plants

These are more advanced than seaweeds, particularly because of their more complex structure, and their ability to produce flowers and seeds. Few have colonized the seashore, let alone the sea. One group of grasses, the eelgrasses, has adapted to genuine marine life, while a small number of other flowering plants can withstand inundation at times.

Lichens

These are extraordinary in that each species is a consistent association of two quite different types of life form – a seaweed and a fungus. They can survive in a wide range of conditions, including those occurring on seashores. Several species are abundant just above the high-water mark, while a few have colonized the inundated parts of the shore.

SEASHORE ANIMALS

Porifera/Sponges

The sponges are simple primitive animals lacking much specialization of cells or structures. They consist basically of a chamber with a large opening, and extract food and oxygen from the sea water that is drawn in through many smaller openings. Varying enormously in size, shape and colour, even within one species, they are notoriously difficult to identify.

Scyphozoa/Jellyfishes

The jellyfishes are part of a larger group of organisms, the Cnidaria, which includes the sea-anemones (opposite). One particular phase of their complex life cycle is dominant – that is the large free-swimming creature known as the medusa. This produces eggs and sperm that give rise to tiny polyps, which attach themselves to a rock or other substrate. When they mature they produce a series of small free-swimming medusae that eventually grow into 'jellyfishes'. They feed by catching prey with their long stinging tentacles. Apart from the small stalked jellyfishes, most are free swimming, and are only found on the shore if they have been washed up.

Anthozoa/Sea-anemones

These are quite primitive and simple, with a bag-like chamber into which the stinging tentacles push prey, although they also depend on planktonic animals that move in with sea water. The stinging tentacles can paralyze prey, but do not have any effect on humans. Sea-anemones occur in a wide variety of forms, mostly brightly coloured, with shapes that often resemble flowers.

Polychaeta/Bristle Worms

The Polychaeta are part of the large group of segmented worms, and many of them look like terrestial worms. They are extremely varied in structure.

Mollusca/Molluscs

This is a very large group of soft-bodied animals that almost always protect themselves in shells – all the animals normally referred to as seashells are molluscs, except for barnacles, which are crustaceans. They are relatively easy to identify compared with most seashore organisms. Five main distinct groups of mollusc are found on the seashores of northern Europe: the chitons, gastropods, bivalves, tusk shells (scaphopods) and cephalopods.

Chitons Also known as coat-of-mail shells, chitons are inconspicuous creatures with a shell made up of calcareous plates, so they look rather like legless woodlice.

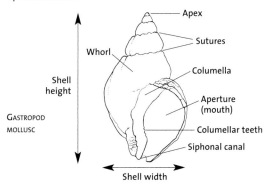

GASTROPOD MOLLUSC

Gastropods These are the largest class of mollusc, with thousands of species. They are characterized by a single, often spiralled shell, except for the curious shell-less sea slugs. They include limpets, ormers, periwinkles, dogwhelks and the sea-slug and its relatives.

Bivalves In these molluscs the shell is divided into two equal halves – they are bilaterally symmetrical. They include mussels, cockles, razor shells and otter shells. In life, the valves of the shell are held shut when necessary by strong muscles, then opened to feed. Some species feed with the aid of a siphon, extracting food and oxygen from the sea water.

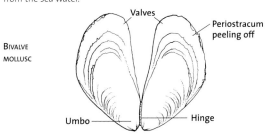

BIVALVE MOLLUSC

Scaphopods Also known as tusk shells, the scaphopods are a small and specialized group of mollusc with elongated tusk-like shells, which live partly buried in sand or mud.

Cephalopods These are superficially quite unlike other molluscs. They are mobile and predatory, with no external shell, and include octopuses, cuttlefish and squid. Most are marine rather than shore animals. The familiar cuttle-bones are the washed-up internal shells of dead cuttlefish.

Crustacea/Crustaceans

These are members of the huge phylum of arthropods (which includes the insects), and are more advanced than the preceding groups. They generally have a clearly defined head, thorax and abdomen, although the barnacles are rather different, and were only seen to be related to the crustaceans because of their similar life history. Crabs, lobsters and prawns are more typical crustaceans, and belong to the decapod order of crustaceans.

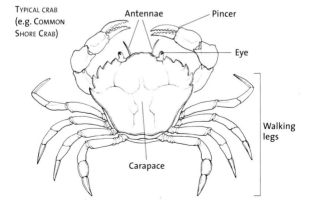

TYPICAL CRAB
(e.g. COMMON
SHORE CRAB)

Antennae

Pincer

Eye

Walking
legs

Carapace

Insecta/Insects
Very few insects have colonized the sea or seashore, despite the huge number of terrestial species. Insects characteristically have a head, thorax and abdomen, and six legs. The primitive springtails and bristle-tails are common on the seashore, together with more mobile insects such as flies that scavenge when the tide is out.

Pycnogonida/Sea-spiders
A small group of entirely marine arthropods resembling terrestial spiders, but not closely related to them despite possessing eight long legs (like spiders).

Echinodermata/Spiny-skinned Animals
This phylum includes the starfishes, brittle stars, feather stars and sea-urchins. They are a distinctive wholly marine group with symmetrical bodies that are either spherical or disc-shaped as in the sea-urchins, or five-star-shaped. Some groups are aggressively predatory, while others, like most sea-urchins, browse on organic material on rocks.

Osteichthyes/Bony Fishes
These fishes form one group of the huge number of fishes. Relatively few occur on the seashore, though a number of smaller fishes, such as gobies, live in rock pools, and others may become stranded.

Birds
Many birds depend on the abundance of the sea for their lives. Numerous birds such as waders inhabit the coasts as residents. Other birds live on coasts just briefly in the mating season, during migration or seasonally, as in the case of many terns and gulls.

Mammals
Relatively few mammals benefit directly from coasts. In northern Europe Eurasian Otters hunt mainly for fish in a number of locations along the shoreline and deeper rock pools. The large and distinctive Common and Grey Seals are the other mammals that are present

on northern European coasts; several thousand can be found around the shores of Britain and Ireland.

Conserving the Seashore

Increasing numbers of people are able to go to coasts for their holidays, and steadily increasing boat traffic leads to increased oil spillage, more rubbish washing up on beaches and a rising level of pollution. All these factors and many more affect the quality of life in the seas and on beaches. When visiting the seashore it is important to follow some basic rules to ensure the conservation of the sea life inhabiting the shore. You can turn rocks over to look for animals, but make sure you put them back in the same place and the right way up. Be very gentle if you pick anything up. Do not pull seaweed off rocks, or remove limpets. Take your litter and only your litter with you – leave all sea creatures where you found them. Wash your hands before eating anything afterwards.

Thankfully pollution incidents are rare, but if you should find a live oiled bird, report it to the Royal Society for the Prevention of Cruelty to Animals (RSPCA). A seal pup on its own is not necessarily in need of rescue – its mother may be out at sea finding food. Watch it but by no means approach it, since any intervention on your part may result in the mother abandoning it, so that it will then need rescuing. If you find live whales, dolphins, porpoises or seals clearly in distress report them to British Divers Marine Life Rescue (BDMLR). If you find dead cetaceans or seals, report them to your local Wildlife Trust.

Safety on the Seashore

The tide can advance very rapidly, particularly over gently shelving beaches, so it is important to know the time of low tide and to check your return route. An innocent-seeming depression can quickly turn into an impassable barrier in areas where there is a marked tidal range. Also do not get too close too cliffs, and keep away from soft mud and quicksand.

You may need to beware of sudden larger waves that can overbalance you on slippery rocks. Make sure you wear suitable footwear to protect you from sharp stones and other hazards.

Green Hairweed
Chaetomorpha linum

SIZE AND DESCRIPTION Length to 10cm. Distinctive though rather inconspicuous green alga consisting of tufts of fine unbranched threads up to 30cm long. No obvious holdfast, but usually grows attached to a solid rocky base in a mass. Strands are soft rather than wiry, and colour is bright green.

HABITAT AND ECOLOGY Very common in pools on the upper and middle shores, extending into fresher water, for example where a stream meets the sea. Most visible in spring and summer.

DISTRIBUTION Occurs widely in the Mediterranean, Atlantic, English Channel, North Sea and Baltic.

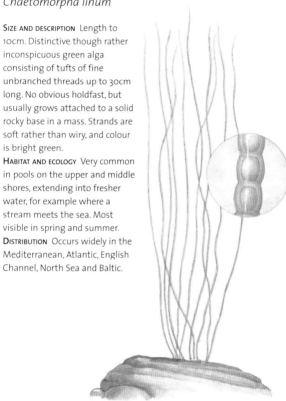

Grass Kelp
Enteromorpha intestinalis

SIZE AND DESCRIPTION Length to 1m.
Well-known and distinctive pale
to bright green alga notable for
its long unbranched cylindrical
fronds, which are inflated by gas-
filled bubbles at intervals, thus
resembling a section of gut.
Fronds may reach 1m, though
they are usually not as long as
this. One of about 10 related
species in European seas. Also
called Gut Weed.

HABITAT AND ECOLOGY Frequently
forms slippery masses on the
upper shore, in varying
situations. Withstands some
degree of pollution, particularly
where there are high nutrient
levels. Especially common in
estuaries. Most conspicuous in
late winter/early spring, when
growth is strongest, dying and
bleaching by late summer.

DISTRIBUTION Very common in
all European seas.

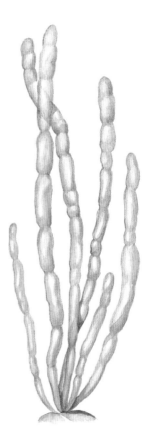

Hen Pen
Bryopsis plumosa

SIZE AND DESCRIPTION Length to 12cm. Small but distinctive glossy green alga with branched feathery fronds arranged in a single plane, and usually growing in tufts. Also called Sea-moss because of its resemblance to some mosses.

HABITAT AND ECOLOGY Quite common on rocky shores, although inconspicuous and easily overlooked. Usually grows in shadier parts of pools on the middle and lower shores, often under overhangs or among larger weeds. Most frequent and visible in spring and summer. Edible, though rather small.

DISTRIBUTION Widespread across Europe.

Sea Lettuce
Ulva lactuca

Size and description Length 10–50cm. Aptly named alga for its clusters of broad leaf-like green fronds, which can resemble miniature lettuces. Shape can vary widely. Fronds are very bright green and translucent, sometimes with white patches where spores have been released. There is always a short stalk. Several related species.
Habitat and ecology Very abundant on rocky shores at lower levels, especially where nutrient levels are high, for example where there is sewage pollution. Visible throughout the year in milder areas; most abundant in July and August. Widely eaten.
Distribution Occurs throughout Europe.

Green alga
Prasiola stipitata

SIZE AND DESCRIPTION Length to 3cm. Small green alga that usually grows in extensive slippery masses on the upper shore. Individual fronds are generally 10–20mm long, of which half is the stalk and the remainder is oblong with curly edges, though variable according to habitat. Alga becomes conspicuous because it grows in quantity.

HABITAT AND ECOLOGY Favourite habitat is rocks at the upper shore level, especially where nutrient levels are high or in areas where there is slight pollution.

DISTRIBUTION Common in the Atlantic, English Channel and North Sea, but not the Mediterranean.

Green alga
Cladophora rupestris

SIZE AND DESCRIPTION
Length to 12cm.
Densely tufted dark
green alga with masses
of short and rather wiry
fronds. Individual fronds
are usually irregularly
branched, and occasionally
opposite. Appears less tufted when out of water. There are several
other species of *Cladophora* in northern and central Europe.
HABITAT AND ECOLOGY Grows on rocks and other solid substrates on
the middle to lower shore, especially under larger brown algae
such as wracks. Dies back in winter, although is still visible; most
conspicuous in summer.
DISTRIBUTION Common in the Atlantic, English Channel, North Sea
and Baltic.

Green alga
Monostroma grevillei

SIZE AND DESCRIPTION Length 10–20cm. Small bright green alga similar to Sea Lettuce (page 21), but distinctly funnel shaped with a split down one side. When out of water, it collapses to look less distinctive, but the shape can be readily seen on closer examination. Fronds are only a cell thick, while those of Sea Lettuce are two cells thick. Several similar species.

HABITAT AND ECOLOGY Widespread in rock pools and on rock platforms from the lower middle shore down to shallow water.

DISTRIBUTION Occurs in the Atlantic, English Channel, North Sea and Baltic, but not the Mediterranean.

Velvet Horn
Codium tomentosum

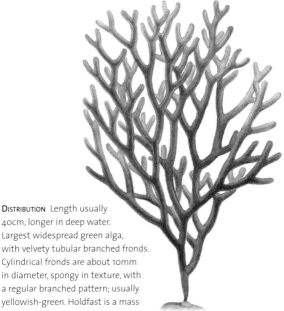

Distribution Length usually 40cm, longer in deep water. Largest widespread green alga, with velvety tubular branched fronds. Cylindrical fronds are about 10mm in diameter, spongy in texture, with a regular branched pattern; usually yellowish-green. Holdfast is a mass of closely woven filaments attached to rock. Several related species, although none looks similar.

Habitat and ecology Occurs from the middle shore down to deep water; most often seen in lower shore rock pools, or washed up. Perennial, with maximum growth in winter.

Distribution Found from the English Channel southwards to the Mediterranean, avoiding colder areas and low salinity.

Brown alga
Punctaria latifolia

SIZE AND DESCRIPTION Length to 40cm. Consists of simple undivided blades measuring 7–8cm across, distinctly greenish in colour and with darker spots and hairs; they may be blunt or pointed at the tips. Several similar species.

HABITAT AND ECOLOGY Widespread on rocks, stones and shells, including live limpets, from the middle shore down to shallow water.

DISTRIBUTION Occurs in the Atlantic, English Channel and North Sea.

Maiden's Hair
Ectocarpus siliculosus

SIZE AND DESCRIPTION Length
to 30cm. Small and untidy-
looking alga consisting of
masses of fine tangled
branches, becoming free
towards the ends. Fronds
are yellow-brown to green-
brown. One of many
species of *Ectocarpus*.
HABITAT AND ECOLOGY Grows
commonly on rocks, smaller
stones and other algae,
from the middle shore
down to shallow water.
DISTRIBUTION Occurs in the
Atlantic, English Channel,
North Sea, Baltic and
Mediterranean.

Kelp
Laminaria digitata

SIZE AND DESCRIPTION
Length 1–4m.
Familiar large brown
alga consisting of a
strong stalk and a broad
fan-like blade made up
of numerous strap-like
sections. Stalk is flexible,
and oval in cross-section. Edible.
Also called Oarweed or Tangle.
HABITAT AND ECOLOGY Grows in masses
at the lowest tidal level and below on
rocky shores, with 'forests' of it exposed
at the lowest tides. Attaches to rock by a
bunch of strong root-like processes that
form a holdfast. Occurs year round.
DISTRIBUTION Common and
widespread in cooler waters
of the Atlantic, English Channel,
North Sea and Baltic.

Sugar Kelp
Laminaria saccharina

SIZE AND DESCRIPTION Length to 3m.
Distinctive and familiar alga consisting
of a single long belt-like frond. Yellowish-
brown to pure brown, with a short stalk that
widens into a convoluted blade. When dry,
crystals of a sugary substance, mannitol, are
visible on its surface. Edible. Also called Poor
Man's Weatherglass.

HABITAT AND ECOLOGY Common in rocky areas,
where it grows attached to various solid
objects, from the lowest shore
downwards. Often washed up.

DISTRIBUTION Grows in cold clear
waters in the Atlantic, English
Channel and North Sea.

Dabberlocks
Alaria esculenta

SIZE AND DESCRIPTION Length 2m or more. Long and strap-like brown alga with a distinctive midrib along the whole length of the blade. Fronds are more delicate and often greener than those of kelps, which lack the midrib. Often becomes torn and tattered after rough weather. Short basal stalk bears groups of lobe-shaped leaves (sporophylls), which carry reproductive organs.

HABITAT AND ECOLOGY A cold-water species growing commonly on exposed rocky shores, where it survives heavy wave battering, despite its delicate appearance.

DISTRIBUTION Grows in the North Sea and on northern Atlantic coasts.

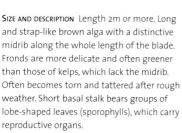

Furbelows
Saccorhiza polyschides

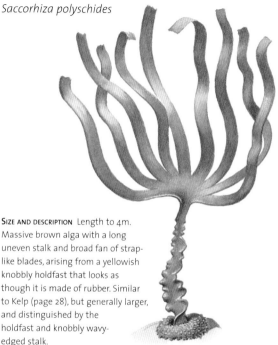

SIZE AND DESCRIPTION Length to 4m.
Massive brown alga with a long
uneven stalk and broad fan of strap-
like blades, arising from a yellowish
knobbly holdfast that looks as
though it is made of rubber. Similar
to Kelp (page 28), but generally larger,
and distinguished by the
holdfast and knobbly wavy-
edged stalk.

HABITAT AND ECOLOGY Widespread and frequent on rocky shores at
the lowest levels. Usually grows in deeper water than Kelp (though
annual, and often washed up after late-autumn gales). More
frequently found in small quantities, rather than in 'forests'.

DISTRIBUTION Grows in the Atlantic, English Channel and North Sea.

Sea Potato
Leathesia difformis

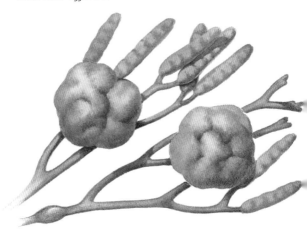

Size and description Diameter 2–5cm (lumps). Brown alga consisting of strange-looking, rounded, olive-brown knobbly lumps, growing on rocks and other algae. Lumps are solid when young, becoming hollow as they age, with the thin branching filaments visible inside.

Habitat and ecology Occurs on the middle and lower shores. First appears in spring, becomes very common in midsummer and disappears by autumn.

Distribution Widely distributed in the Atlantic, English Channel and North Sea.

Beanweed
Scytosiphon lomentaria

SIZE AND DESCRIPTION Length to
30cm. Somewhat resembles a
long and narrow string of slimy
greenish sausages. Greenish or
yellowish-brown fronds are
tubular and unbranched with gas
bladders at intervals, divided by
constrictions. Edible and reputed
to taste of beans, hence its
common name.

HABITAT AND ECOLOGY Very common
and often abundant in both
rocky and stony areas, growing
on every kind of substrate from
the middle shore downwards
into shallow water. Most
conspicuous in winter, except
in the coldest areas.

DISTRIBUTION Occurs from the
Atlantic and Baltic, to the
Mediterranean.

Bootlace Weed
Chorda filum

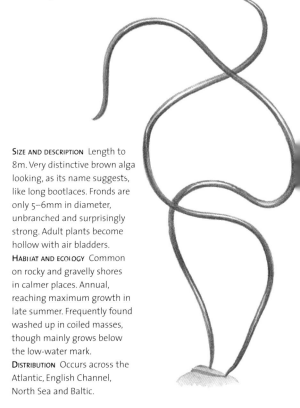

SIZE AND DESCRIPTION Length to 8m. Very distinctive brown alga looking, as its name suggests, like long bootlaces. Fronds are only 5–6mm in diameter, unbranched and surprisingly strong. Adult plants become hollow with air bladders.

HABITAT AND ECOLOGY Common on rocky and gravelly shores in calmer places. Annual, reaching maximum growth in late summer. Frequently found washed up in coiled masses, though mainly grows below the low-water mark.

DISTRIBUTION Occurs across the Atlantic, English Channel, North Sea and Baltic.

Brown alga
Bifurcaria bifurcaria

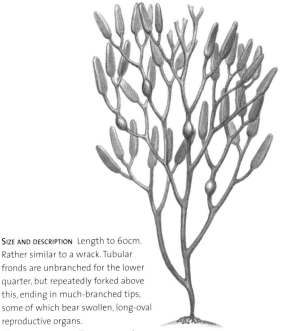

SIZE AND DESCRIPTION Length to 60cm. Rather similar to a wrack. Tubular fronds are unbranched for the lower quarter, but repeatedly forked above this, ending in much-branched tips, some of which bear swollen, long-oval reproductive organs.

HABITAT AND ECOLOGY Occurs on rock and in rock pools on the lower shore, but is not normally found exposed to the air (unlike the wracks).

DISTRIBUTION Mainly an Atlantic species, occurring around southern and south-western Britain.

Sea Sorrel
Desmarestia ligulata

SIZE AND DESCRIPTION Length to 1.5m. Belongs to a group of much-branched fern-like species. Numerous branched fronds are roughly triangular in outline and carried on a central stem. They are tufted with fine hairs in summer, and olive-brown when alive and submerged, but soon turn green and flabby out of water. There are several related species.

HABITAT AND ECOLOGY Found in rocky areas and in pools, from the lower shore down to shallow water. Often washed up. Contains sulphuric acid and tends to bleach other algae growing next to it.

DISTRIBUTION Occurs in waters of the Atlantic and English Channel.

Sea Oak
Halidrys siliquosa

SIZE AND DESCRIPTION Length to 1m. Much-branched robust brown alga. Fronds have numerous uneven branches, and are stiff and leathery in texture, and slightly greenish. Air bladders on the ends of the branches are divided internally into chambers and resemble seedpods of the mustard family; the largest bladders have long sharp points.

HABITAT AND ECOLOGY Occurs on rocks on the lower shore and in shallow water, extending higher up the shore in sheltered places.

DISTRIBUTION Widespread in the Atlantic, English Channel and North Sea, though rarely common.

Peacock's Tail
Padina pavonia

SIZE AND DESCRIPTION Length to 10cm. Unusual little species consisting of robust, fan-shaped and upright silvery fronds, which have a greenish tinge inside and brown stripes on the outside. Fronds are triangular in form, narrowing down to the holdfast, but maintaining a roughly funnel-shaped structure.

HABITAT AND ECOLOGY Widespread though rarely common in warmer waters on rocky shores, in shallow water and in rock pools on the lower shore.

DISTRIBUTION Found from the southern coasts of Britain southwards to the Mediterranean.

Rainbow Bladder Weed
Cystoseira tamariscifolia

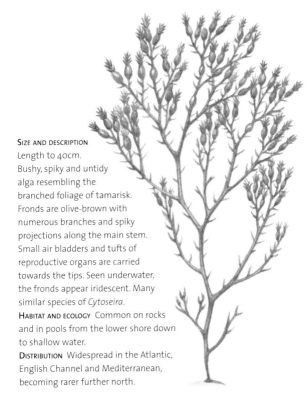

SIZE AND DESCRIPTION
Length to 40cm.
Bushy, spiky and untidy
alga resembling the
branched foliage of tamarisk.
Fronds are olive-brown with
numerous branches and spiky
projections along the main stem.
Small air bladders and tufts of
reproductive organs are carried
towards the tips. Seen underwater,
the fronds appear iridescent. Many
similar species of *Cytoseira*.

HABITAT AND ECOLOGY Common on rocks
and in pools from the lower shore down
to shallow water.

DISTRIBUTION Widespread in the Atlantic,
English Channel and Mediterranean,
becoming rarer further north.

Thongweed
Himanthalia elongata

SIZE AND DESCRIPTION Length to 2m. Long, branched, narrow and strap-shaped fronds arise from small and toadstool-shaped structures surmounting the holdfast. Fronds branch evenly, though only by a limited amount. The curious olive-green 'toadstool' structures may often be found without the main frond. Similar to Bootlace Weed (page 34), although this is unbranched, cylindrical and lacks the 'toadstools'.

HABITAT AND ECOLOGY Common in exposed rocky areas from the lower shore down to shallow water, and in rock pools.

DISTRIBUTION Occurs in the waters of the Atlantic and English Channel.

Japweed
Sargassum muticum

SIZE AND DESCRIPTION Length to 5m. Recognizable by its enormous length. Slender main stem that branches alternately. Leaves are small and lance shaped, and the gas bladders are spherical.

HABITAT AND ECOLOGY Occurs on the middle to lower shore, often in rock pools, where its growth may be prodigious. Only relatively recently found in Britain, on the south coast, but has spread rapidly, especially westwards, and can be very abundant in sheltered areas. An invasive species, it overgrows and chokes native animals and plants, and can cause fouling problems in anchorages.

DISTRIBUTION Locally abundant on southern coasts of Britain and Atlantic coasts of France. Native to the Pacific.

Wrack
Fucus ceranoides

SIZE AND DESCRIPTION Length to 60cm. Undistinguished wrack with regularly branched fronds and clusters of small branched reproductive bodies at the tips. Greenish-brown fronds are usually smaller than those of other wracks.

HABITAT AND ECOLOGY Most common in brackish water – rather than strongly salty water – like that found in estuaries, where it grows commonly on rock, stones and gravel at all shore levels.

DISTRIBUTION Occurs in the Atlantic, English Channel and North Sea.

Knotted Wrack
Ascophyllum nodosum

SIZE AND DESCRIPTION Length to 1.5m.
Untidy brown alga with egg-
shaped bladders along the
stems. Bladders do not 'pop' like
those of Bladderwrack (page
45), and in other respects
look quite different.
Fronds branch repeatedly
and unevenly. There are
separate male and female
plants, with each
producing raisin-like
fruiting bodies that are
yellow in male, greenish
in female.
HABITAT AND ECOLOGY
Extremely common on
sheltered rocky shores,
blanketing rocks in the
right conditions, though
very stunted where exposure
is too great.
DISTRIBUTION Occurs in the
Atlantic, English Channel
and North Sea.

Toothed Wrack
Fucus serratus

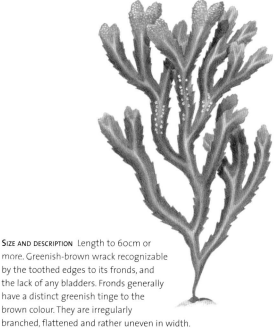

SIZE AND DESCRIPTION Length to 60cm or more. Greenish-brown wrack recognizable by the toothed edges to its fronds, and the lack of any bladders. Fronds generally have a distinct greenish tinge to the brown colour. They are irregularly branched, flattened and rather uneven in width.

HABITAT AND ECOLOGY Occurs, often abundantly, in a distinct zone on the lower to middle section of rocky shore, with only short exposure to air. Provides homes and shelter for numerous other species.

DISTRIBUTION Widespread throughout colder water areas in the Atlantic, English Channel, North Sea and Baltic.

Bladderwrack
Fucus vesiculosus

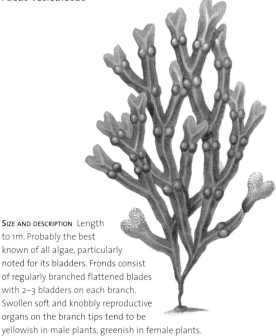

SIZE AND DESCRIPTION Length
to 1m. Probably the best
known of all algae, particularly
noted for its bladders. Fronds consist
of regularly branched flattened blades
with 2–3 bladders on each branch.
Swollen soft and knobbly reproductive
organs on the branch tips tend to be
yellowish in male plants, greenish in female plants.

HABITAT AND ECOLOGY Very common and widespread on rocky shores
in cold-water areas, growing in a distinct zone on the middle shore,
but not on very exposed sites.

DISTRIBUTION Occurs throughout the Atlantic, English Channel, North
Sea and Baltic.

Channelled Wrack
Pelvetia canaliculata

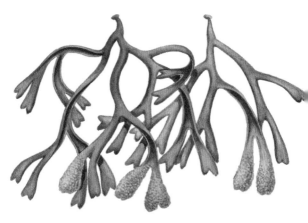

SIZE AND DESCRIPTION Length to 15cm. Brown wrack with markedly grooved fronds. These are short, and their tips may be swollen with the typical wrack reproductive organs.

HABITAT AND ECOLOGY A very common species forming a distinct zone on the upper parts of rocky shores, even extending above the high-water mark. Where not submerged but regularly wetted by spray, it tends to be slender, brittle and blackish. Cattle and sheep feed on this alga, hence its alternate name of Cow Tang.

DISTRIBUTION Occurs in the Atlantic, English Channel and North Sea.

Spiral Wrack
Fucus spiralis

SIZE AND DESCRIPTION
Length to 40cm.
Typical brown wrack, rather
similar to Bladderwrack
(page 45), but distinguished
by its twisted fronds, lack of
bladders and conspicuous
reproductive bodies. Branched
fronds are greenish-brown,
sometimes yellowish. Midrib is
strongly marked, and the tips of
the branches are swollen with the reproductive organs, which do not
reach the edge of the frond and are surrounded by a strip of flat blade.
HABITAT AND ECOLOGY Common on the upper zone of rocky shores, away
from exposed areas.
DISTRIBUTION Occurs throughout northern parts.

Sea Noodle
Nemalion helminthoides

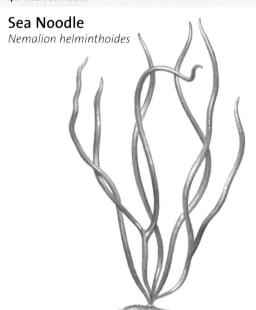

Size and description Length to 25cm. Red alga looking rather like a cluster of curly spaghetti. Individual fronds are cylindrical and worm-like, and about 2cm in diameter. Some forms only branch once at the base, others throughout their length. They vary in colour from red to purplish-brown.

Habitat and ecology Locally common on the lower shore and in rock pools, on exposed rocky shores.

Distribution Occurs mainly in the Atlantic; infrequent in the North Sea and rare in the Baltic.

Landlady's Wig
Ahnfeltia plicata

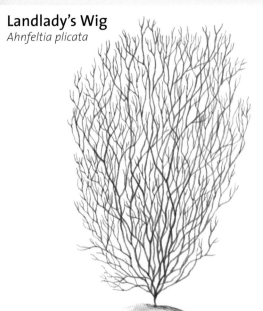

SIZE AND DESCRIPTION Length to 15cm. Wiry tufted species consisting of clusters of dark red fronds. Texture of this alga has been described as being 'like a lump of two-amp fuse wire', and differentiates it from similar-looking species. Fronds have many branches, in tufts that are about 10cm across, of a dark red that is nearly black.

HABITAT AND ECOLOGY Occurs in rock pools and rocky areas from the middle shore down to shallow water.

DISTRIBUTION Widely distributed and locally common in the Atlantic, English Channel and North Sea.

Coral Weed
Corallina officinalis

SIZE AND DESCRIPTION Length to 12cm. Fern-like red alga with calcified fronds that turn white as they die. Individual fronds are notable for their regular branching, every branch or branchlet having an exact opposite. Main branches are made up of tiny articulated sections. Original reddish-plum colour fades as the plant ages or is exposed to the sun, turning yellow, then white. There are several related species.

HABITAT AND ECOLOGY Common on the middle shore, particularly as a fringe around rock pools just below water level.

DISTRIBUTION Widespread in the Atlantic, English Channel, North Sea and Mediterranean; rare in the Baltic.

Sea Beech
Delesseria sanguinea

SIZE AND DESCRIPTION Length to 40cm. Resembles a bunch of reddish-brown leaves fallen from a tree. Bright translucent red frond consists of a short main stem dividing into a number of leaf-like branches, each with midribs and side veins, and wavy margins. Fronds disintegrate late in the year, and small spore-bearing outgrowths develop along the midrib.

HABITAT AND ECOLOGY Common on rocks and larger seaweeds on the lower shore, mainly in deep shady pools, where it occurs as isolated plants.

DISTRIBUTION Found in the Atlantic, English Channel and North Sea; rare in the Baltic.

Batter Frond
Gigartina stellata

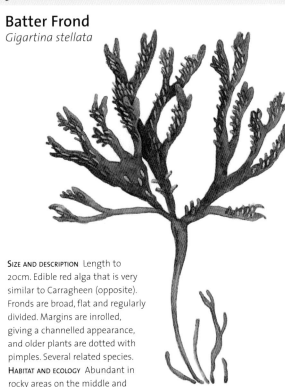

SIZE AND DESCRIPTION Length to 20cm. Edible red alga that is very similar to Carragheen (opposite). Fronds are broad, flat and regularly divided. Margins are inrolled, giving a channelled appearance, and older plants are dotted with pimples. Several related species.

HABITAT AND ECOLOGY Abundant in rocky areas on the middle and lower shores, sometimes forming a band at the lower level. Grows on rocks and stones, and in rock pools.

DISTRIBUTION Widespread in the Atlantic, English Channel and North Sea, and most common in the west.

Carragheen
Chondrus crispus

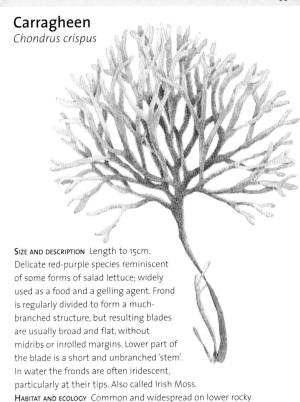

Size and description Length to 15cm.
Delicate red-purple species reminiscent
of some forms of salad lettuce; widely
used as a food and a gelling agent. Frond
is regularly divided to form a much-
branched structure, but resulting blades
are usually broad and flat, without
midribs or inrolled margins. Lower part of
the blade is a short and unbranched 'stem'.
In water the fronds are often iridescent,
particularly at their tips. Also called Irish Moss.
Habitat and ecology Common and widespread on lower rocky
shores, in shallow water and occasionally in pools.
Distribution Occurs in the Atlantic, English Channel and North Sea,
and rarely in the Baltic.

Pepper Dulse
Laurencia pinnatifida

SIZE AND DESCRIPTION Length to 12cm. Attractive small and inconspicuous alga, which is edible. Individual reddish to yellowish-brown fronds have a strong main stem divided on either side into branches like the rungs of a ladder, which are further divided into finer tufts at the ends. Related species with different branching patterns occur.

HABITAT AND ECOLOGY Grows in clusters on rocks and in crevices from the middle shore down to shallow water.

DISTRIBUTION Widespread and locally common in the Atlantic, English Channel and North Sea.

Dulse
Rhodymenia palmata

Size and description Length to 30cm. Rather amorphous alga that is well known as an edible and medicinal species. Consists of a cluster of broad and flat divided blades. Individual fronds are broad, flat and thick, widening out from a very short or non-existent stalk, and red-crimson in colour.

Habitat and ecology Common mainly in rocky areas on the middle and lower shores, extending to below the lowest spring-tide mark, attached to rocks, stones and large brown seaweeds, particularly species of the *Laminaria* genus.

Distribution Widespread in the Atlantic, English Channel and North Sea.

Laver
Porphyra umbilicalis

SIZE AND DESCRIPTION Length to 20cm. Well-known edible alga, most distinctive when seen growing in extensive silky, leafy masses over rocks. Individual fronds can be hard to distinguish from the mass. They are delicate and membranous, lobed like leaves and form irregular groups. Frond colour is green or dark rosy-red when young, turning to olive-green to dark brown or purple-brown with age. Laver growing on the upper shore and exposed by the tide for some time may be partially dried out, black and crispy. It is eaten as a delicacy, particularly in Wales. Several related species, all edible.

HABITAT AND ECOLOGY Locally common on exposed beaches that are both sandy and rocky.

DISTRIBUTION Occurs in the Atlantic, English Channel, North Sea and Mediterranean.

Eelgrass
Zostera spp.

SIZE AND DESCRIPTION Length to 1m. Grass-like flowering plant that has become totally marine. Eelgrasses have leaves typical of grasses and their relatives – long and thin, with a series of parallel veins. There are separate male and female plants, each producing different flowers.

HABITAT AND ECOLOGY Two species of eelgrass (*Z. angustifolia* and *Z. noltii*) occur mainly in sheltered waters of estuaries from the middle shore down to shallow water. A third species (*Z. marina*) grows on muddy and sandy beaches from the lowest tide levels down to about 4m, and is thus rarely seen. All species of eelgrass flower from mid to late summer.

DISTRIBUTION Found throughout Europe.

Sea Purslane
Halimione portulacoides

SIZE AND DESCRIPTION Height to 80cm. Small flowering evergreen shrub with greyish mealy leaves. Flowers are individually insignificant, but yellowish-green spikes are noticeable en masse in June–September.

HABITAT AND ECOLOGY Occurs commonly around the tops of salt marshes and along creeks, often forming a distinct zone. Well known as a hiding place for crabs, hence its alternate name of Crab-grass.

DISTRIBUTION Common and frequently abundant in suitable sheltered sites across Europe.

Common Cord-grass
Spartina anglica

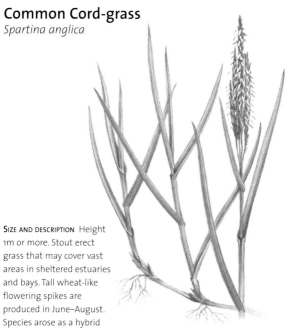

SIZE AND DESCRIPTION Height 1m or more. Stout erect grass that may cover vast areas in sheltered estuaries and bays. Tall wheat-like flowering spikes are produced in June–August. Species arose as a hybrid between two more slender and rarer *Spartina* species (*S. maritima* and *S. alternifolia*), but is now accepted as a species itself.

HABITAT AND ECOLOGY More aggressive than its parents, and colonizes further into deeper water, often ousting more demanding salt-marsh species. Widely used as a mud binder to reclaim tidal land, which it raises by trapping silt.

DISTRIBUTION Widespread and common in the majority of areas, and often introduced.

Marsh Samphire
Salicornia europaea

SIZE AND DESCRIPTION Height to 30cm. Erect flowering plant with shiny succulent jointed stems bearing numerous shorter side branches all around. Dark green at first, becoming yellowish-green and eventually reddish and woody when in fruit, dying back completely by late autumn. Also called Glasswort. A number of related species in Europe.

HABITAT AND ECOLOGY Grows in extensive masses on mudflats, and in salt marshes and estuaries.

DISTRIBUTION Occurs in suitable coastal locations in much of Europe.

Sea-holly
Eryngium maritimum

SIZE AND DESCRIPTION
Height to 60cm.
Striking architectural
perennial. Leaves are
bluish-green, leathery
and ovate, with sharp
spines that give them
a holly-like appearance.
Basal leaves are stalked,
while stem leaves are
stalkless. Flowers are small
and purple-blue, appearing
in June–September. They are packed into rounded teasel-like heads
borne with spiny bracts below, and attract bees and butterflies.
Roots were once pulped, sugared and sold as sweets.

HABITAT AND ECOLOGY Grows in stable and undisturbed coastal sand
and shingle.

DISTRIBUTION Widespread in suitable areas on European coasts.

Lovage
Ligusticum scoticum

SIZE AND DESCRIPTION Height to 60cm. Perennial with thick stems and a substantial rhizome. Leaves are large and divided into three leaflets, which are again divided into three segments, with diamond-shaped lobes and toothed margins. White flowers are borne in dense compound umbels 4–6cm across in June–July.

HABITAT AND ECOLOGY
Grows in shingle, sand dunes and rocky outcrops along the seashore and on sea cliffs.

DISTRIBUTION Locally common along the coasts of Scotland, Northern Ireland and northern Europe as far as Norway.

Oysterplant
Mertensia maritima

SIZE AND DESCRIPTION Height to
60cm. Sprawling perennial with
fleshy bluish-grey leaf stems.
Leaves are up to 6cm long, spoon
shaped or pointed. Lower leaves
are stalked, upper leaves
stalkless. Funnel-shaped
flowers are 6mm across,
borne in terminal
clusters in June–August,
and pink at first,
becoming pale blue.
Also called Sea Lungwort.
HABITAT AND ECOLOGY Grows
on sand and shingle beaches
around the high-tide mark.
DISTRIBUTION Locally distributed
on the Atlantic coasts of
northern Britain and Ireland,
and the coast of continental
Europe from Jutland
northwards.

Rock Samphire
Crithmum maritimum

SIZE AND DESCRIPTION
Height to 50cm.
Perennial that is
woody at the base, and
has fleshy hairless stems
and leaves with straight
fleshy lobes. Flowers are
yellow and borne in
thick-stalked, plate-like
umbels. Fruits are
5–6mm in diameter, yellow or purple, with thick ridges.
HABITAT AND ECOLOGY Grows in coastal areas among rocks and
stabilized shingle.
DISTRIBUTION Occurs on the Atlantic coast of Britain from Scotland
southwards, and from north-west France south, including the
coasts of the Black Sea and Mediterranean.

Alexanders
Smyrnium olusatrum

SIZE AND DESCRIPTION Height to 1.5m. Biennial with celery-scented shiny dark green leaves divided into three, each segment being three lobed with a toothed margin. Flowers are yellow with up to 15 simple umbels forming a compound umbel.
Fruits are up to 6mm in diameter, oval, hard and reddish-brown.

HABITAT AND ECOLOGY Grows in sandy soils, often near the sea.

DISTRIBUTION Naturalized and common around the coasts of southern Britain and continental Europe, northwards to Denmark.

Sea Kale
Crambe maritima

SIZE AND DESCRIPTION Height to 75cm. Architectural perennial with a branched fleshy rhizome and a thick erect stem. Leaves are bluish and leathery, lobed with wavy margins. Mature leaves are very large, usually 30–50cm long. Flowers are white, up to 1.5cm in diameter and borne in striking dense terminal clusters in June–August. Plant forms a large and almost hemispherical thicket resting on the ground.

HABITAT AND ECOLOGY Grows on shingle beaches on coasts, in poor calcareous soils.

DISTRIBUTION Widespread but sparsely distributed on the shores of Britain and continental northern Europe.

Common Scurvy-grass
Cochlearia officinalis

SIZE AND DESCRIPTION Height to 30cm. Biennial or perennial with a long taproot. Several smooth and fleshy stems spring from the rootstock and are either trailing or vertical. Basal leaves are heart shaped varying to kidney shaped or round, with long stalks. Stem leaves are stalkless, clasp the stem, and are lobed and toothed. Flowers are small with four white petals, and arranged in loose spikes.

HABITAT AND ECOLOGY Grows in salt marshes, on coastal cliffs, and inland near salt mines and saline springs.

DISTRIBUTION Occurs throughout most European coastal areas. Common in much of Britain.

Sea Beet
Beta vulgaris maritima

SIZE AND DESCRIPTION Height to 80cm. Annual, biennial or perennial, sometimes sprawling, but usually bushy. Leaves are shiny green, oval or wedge-shaped, and pointed. Flowers are small and greenish, arranged in clusters of up to three and borne on a branched spike. The wild ancestor of common vegetables such as beetroot, sugar beet and Swiss chard.

HABITAT AND ECOLOGY Grows on coasts on the edges of salt marshes and along coastal footpaths on calcareous soils.

DISTRIBUTION Found in southern and western Europe, including southern Britain, but rarer further north.

Yellow Horned-poppy
Glaucium flavum

SIZE AND DESCRIPTION
Height to 90cm.
Branching clump-forming
biennial or perennial. Leaves
are blue-green, the basal ones
being deeply pinnately lobed and
arranged in a rosette. Flowers are
6–8cm across and consist of two sepals and four papery bright yellow
petals; they appear in April–September. Horn-like pods are up to 30cm
long, slender and curved.
HABITAT AND ECOLOGY Restricted principally to stable stretches of
coastal shingle.
DISTRIBUTION Occurs on most suitable coasts around Europe, but
generally only locally common.

Green Tar Lichen
Verrucaria mucosa

SIZE AND DESCRIPTION Usually greenish-grey to olive-green lichen, the crust of which attaches very closely to rock. Very similar to Black Tar Lichen (page 72), but the crust is slightly thicker and not cracked into rectangular sections.

HABITAT AND ECOLOGY Occurs in irregular patches on rocks, but only on those below the high-water mark.

DISTRIBUTION Common on the Atlantic and English Channel coasts.

Lichen
Lichina pygmaea

SIZE AND DESCRIPTION Height to 1cm. Upright branching lichen that forms small bushes like a miniature seaweed. Occurs in tiny patches up to a few centimetres across, which are made up of much-divided dark brown to black branches.

HABITAT AND ECOLOGY Found on rocky shores from the high-water mark downwards, so it is regularly immersed.

DISTRIBUTION Common in suitable habitats on the Atlantic, English Channel, North Sea and Mediterranean coasts.

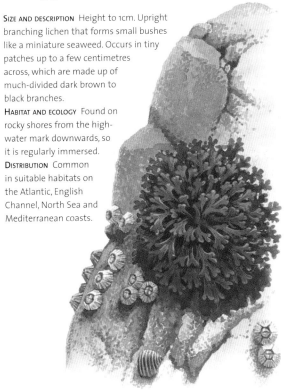

Black Tar Lichen
Verrucaria maura

SIZE AND DESCRIPTION Matt black or greenish-black encrusting lichen that occurs on rocks and boulders in irregularly circular patches. Body is cracked into roughly rectangular sections, sometimes with small conical fruiting bodies. Crust is very thin. Extensive patches are often mistaken for dried-up oil washed up from ships.

HABITAT AND ECOLOGY Very common on rocky coasts from above high water to some way below it. Can cover huge areas, particularly on exposed shores.

DISTRIBUTION Widely distributed in suitable locations around the Atlantic, English Channel and North Sea coasts.

Sulphur Sponge
Suberites domuncula

SIZE AND DESCRIPTION Diameter to 30cm. Fleshy and globular orange-yellow sponge. Very variable, but most commonly roughly spherical, with a smooth texture. If removed from the water it shrinks rapidly.

HABITAT AND ECOLOGY Occurs in clean water from the low-water mark downwards, on rocks, harbour piles, and so on. It has a particular association with whelk shells occupied by hermit crabs, and may eventually dissolve away a shell and form a crab's home directly.

DISTRIBUTION Found in the Atlantic, English Channel, North Sea and Mediterranean.

Breadcrumb Sponge
Halichondria panicea

Size and description Diameter to 25cm. Encrusting body of this sponge varies from white, through orange, to green, depending partly on the degree of colonization of algae, which relates to the light levels. Occurs in irregular rounded areas, usually with characteristic 'craters', but occasionally with more elongated structures.

Habitat and ecology Colonizes rock surfaces, stones and larger algae from the middle shore down to deep water.

Distribution Common and widespread in the Atlantic, English Channel, North Sea, parts of the Baltic and Mediterranean.

Common Jellyfish
Aurelia aurita

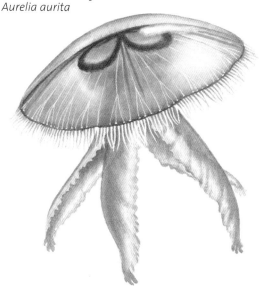

SIZE AND DESCRIPTION Diameter to 25cm. Typical jellyfish, most commonly seen as a dome of transparent jelly washed up on the shore. In this species the 'umbrella' is circular, and there are four conspicuous long purplish mouth-arms hanging below. The crescent-shaped purple reproductive organs are visible within the umbrella.
HABITAT AND ECOLOGY A pelagic floating species that is washed up on beaches according to tides and gales. Large groups may often be found together.
DISTRIBUTION Occurs virtually around the world.

Snakelocks Anemone
Anemonia viridis

SIZE AND DESCRIPTION Length to 12cm. Attractive and distinctive anemone with a mass of long and colourful tentacles that almost hide the short and broad trunk. Tentacles are not fully retractable. They are most commonly green with pink-purple tips, although various other colours occur.

HABITAT AND ECOLOGY Common in clear rocky conditions, from pools on the middle shore downwards. Thrives best in well-lit situations.

DISTRIBUTION Occurs on the Atlantic and Mediterranean coasts, and in the western English Channel.

Beadlet Anemone
Actinia equina

SIZE AND DESCRIPTION Length to 7cm. Common species, familiar as both a closed bob and open with waving tentacles. When open underwater it is about 5–6cm in diameter and to 7cm high, with hundreds of tentacles arranged in rings. When disturbed or out of the water the tentacles can be quickly retracted, and the animal reverts to a blob of jelly about 3cm high. Colour is variable – it is most commonly red-orange, but can also be green or brown. A strawberry form is red with yellowish spots.

HABITAT AND ECOLOGY Very common in rocky areas from the middle shore downwards.

DISTRIBUTION Widespread throughout the Atlantic, English Channel, North Sea and Mediterranean.

Sinistral Spiral Tubeworm
Spirorbis borealis

SIZE AND DESCRIPTION Diameter 3–5mm. Tiny coiled calcareous shells on seaweeds that look more like molluscs than worms. When underwater, the green tentacles of the worms can be seen. The rest of the time they appear as immobile clockwise-coiled white tubes. There are several similar species.

HABITAT AND ECOLOGY Very common and often extremely abundant on the middle and lower shores, on brown seaweeds such as kelps and wracks, as well as on rocks and stones.

DISTRIBUTION Occurs across the Atlantic, English Channel, North Sea and Mediterranean.

Greenleaf Worm
Eulalia viridis

Size and description
Length to 15cm.
Attractive and
conspicuous long, thin
and slow-moving green worm
with paddle-like legs. Body may be
made up of 50–200 segments, and is
bright grass-green. King Rag Worm (*Nereis
virens*) has a similar colour and leg shape, but is usually much larger.
Habitat and ecology Commonly seen creeping around on rocks at low
tide, especially in dull weather, stretching and contracting slowly.
Also lives, often unseen, in rock crevices.
Distribution Common in the Atlantic, English Channel, North Sea,
western Baltic and Mediterranean.

Coat-of-mail Chiton
Lepidopleurus asellus

SIZE AND DESCRIPTION Length to 2cm. Small articulated mollusc resembling a legless woodlouse. Consists of jointed shells made up of eight sections. Usually brown with the margin in the same colour. Many similar species.

HABITAT AND ECOLOGY Found attached to rocks, stones and other hard surfaces from the lower shore down to considerable depths of water. Widespread and common, though easily overlooked.

DISTRIBUTION Occurs in the Atlantic, English Channel and North Sea.

Green Ormer
Haliotis tuberculata

SIZE AND DESCRIPTION Length to 10cm. Large and ear-shaped greenish shell about 4cm across, with a line of holes along one edge, and with further older ones blocked off. Roughly oval, and the upper surface is creased, folded and ridged. Inside is thickly lined with beautiful mother-of-pearl.

HABITAT AND ECOLOGY Occurs strongly attached on rocks and stones from the lower shore down to shallow water.

DISTRIBUTION Found in the Atlantic as far north as the Channel Islands, and in the Mediterranean.

Slit Limpet
Eumarginula reticulata

SIZE AND DESCRIPTION Length to 2cm. Distinctive triangular or conical shell with a slightly turned-over tip and a marked slit down one side. Strongly ribbed, and white or cream. Several similar species.

HABITAT AND ECOLOGY Occurs on rocks and stones from the lower shore down to deep water.

DISTRIBUTION Widespread though not particularly common in the Atlantic, English Channel and North Sea.

Blue-rayed Limpet
Patina pellucida

SIZE AND DESCRIPTION
Length to 2cm. Beautiful little limpet that has strongly marked electric-blue rays across its shell. Oval or pear shaped when seen from above, low and rounded from the side. Distinctive radiating lines of bright blue dots usually emanate from a dark blue spot at the narrower end. Colour and size are variable, according to age.

HABITAT AND ECOLOGY
Usually found attached to *Laminaria* kelp algae rather than to rocks, from the lower shore to moderately deep water.

DISTRIBUTION Common in much of the Atlantic, English Channel and North Sea.

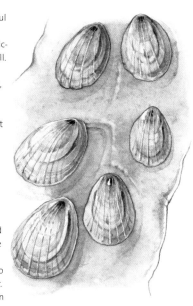

Common Limpet
Patella vulgata

Size and description Length to 7cm. Well-known and abundant species with a conical shell. Irregularly but not strongly ribbed, usually pale cream or grey, not boldly marked and often encrusted with barnacles. Interior is creamy to yellowish with a silvery-brown scar at the apex. There are a number of similar species, including China Limpet (*P. aspera*), which has a bluish interior with an orange headscar.

Habitat and ecology Very common in rocky areas from the upper shore downwards, becoming smaller and flatter further down.

Distribution Occurs in the Atlantic, English Channel and North Sea.

Tortoiseshell Limpet
Acmaea tessulata

SIZE AND DESCRIPTION Length to 2.5cm. Typically shaped limpet with distinctive tortoiseshell marbling on its outer surface. Shell is conical and slightly flattened with strong reddish-brown and white markings. Inside the shell the apex is brown. More delicate than Common Limpet (opposite) and easily recognized. White Tortoiseshell Limpet (*A. virginea*) is considerably smaller, paler and less mottled, but otherwise similar.

HABITAT AND ECOLOGY Common on rocks and stones from the lower shore down to deep water.

DISTRIBUTION Occurs only in northern parts of the region, on the northern Atlantic coasts, and in the North Sea and Baltic.

Keyhole Limpet
Diodora apertura

SIZE AND DESCRIPTION Length to 4cm. One of a small group of limpets with typical conical shells that have a rectangular or rounded opening at the apex. Shell is elongated when seen from above, yellowish or creamy-grey outside, regularly ribbed from the apex, and has a clearly visible 'keyhole' through which a small tube protrudes when the animal is alive and under water.

HABITAT AND ECOLOGY Fairly common on rocks from the lower shore down to moderately deep water.

DISTRIBUTION Occurs in the Atlantic, English Channel and North Sea.

Toothed Winkle
Monodonta lineata

Size and description Height to 3cm. Pointed, conical and coiled shell about 2–3cm wide, with six whorls that may be difficult to interpret. Tip is usually white or grey, and the remainder of the external surface has zigzag markings in reddish-purple, occasionally green, or a mixture of both colours. Mouth has a single projecting tooth in the otherwise smooth lines. Inside is strongly coated with mother-of-pearl. Also called Thick Topshell.

Habitat and ecology Occurs on rocks of the middle shore.

Distribution Locally very common in the Atlantic as far as north Wales, and as far west as the central English Channel.

Common Topshell
Calliostoma zizyphinum

SIZE AND DESCRIPTION Height to 3cm. Attractive conical shell with a
maximum width of 3cm. Sides are very straight with little distinction
between the coils. Surface is yellowish-pink with darker mottling
and pronounced darker dotted stripes spiralling around the shell.
Additionally occurs in white and violet-blue forms. Also called Painted
Topshell. Grooved Topshell (*Cantharidus striatus*) is like a much smaller
version of this species, 1cm high and narrower across.

HABITAT AND ECOLOGY Widely distributed and common on the lower
shore down to deep water.

DISTRIBUTION Occurs across the Atlantic, English Channel, North Sea
and Mediterranean.

Flat Topshell
Gibbula umbilicalis

Size and description Height to 1.5cm. Small conical and coiled shell with a distinctly flattened apex, and up to 2cm across. There are usually seven whorls, and the shell is silvery green-grey with strongly marked red-purple stripes radiating out from the apex down to the mouth. Also called Purple Topshell. Similar species include Grey Topshell (*G. cineraria*).

Habitat and ecology Locally abundant on rocks and stones from the upper shore down to the lower shore. Quite common in upper-shore rock pools.

Distribution Occurs mainly in the south-west of the Atlantic and English Channel.

Flat Periwinkle
Littorina littoralis

SIZE AND DESCRIPTION Height to 1cm. Common and variable shell, rounded in outline and with a flat top. It is small, barely reaching 1cm across, and distinctly compressed downwards so that the mouth reaches almost to the apex. Shell surface is smooth, and usually orange, but also occurs in brown, red, green and occasionally striped forms.

HABITAT AND ECOLOGY Most frequently found moving over the surface of brown algae, especially wracks, on which it grazes. It is active out of the water, unlike many other species.

DISTRIBUTION Occurs in the Atlantic, English Channel, North Sea and western Baltic.

Rough Periwinkle
Littorina saxatilis

Size and description Height to 1.25cm. Variable conical shell with a pointed apex and a rough stripy surface. It is markedly coiled, with 6–9 coils separated by distinct grooves. The curve of the shell opening meets the main spire at a right angle. Colour is variable, but usually orange-red to black, though often appearing rather grey and faded. Shell is distinctly rough to the touch.

Habitat and ecology Usually found in crevices and cracks of rocks, on stones and boulders, and among brown algae on the upper to upper-middle shore. Feeds on algae, and can breathe in air, like Flat Periwinkle (opposite).

Distribution Widespread in the Atlantic, English Channel and North Sea.

Edible Periwinkle
Littorina littorea

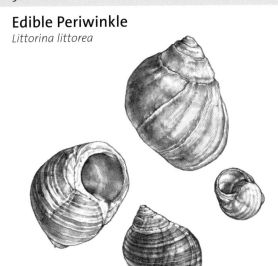

SIZE AND DESCRIPTION Height to 3cm. Large, solid and robust periwinkle with a pointed conical shell. Colour is variable, from red, through grey to black, usually rather dull, though always with some concentric darker striping; often bands and apex of a different colour. Surface is slightly rough to the touch. Small individuals are distinguishable from Rough Periwinkle (page 91) by the narrower angle at which the edge of the opening meets the spire.

HABITAT AND ECOLOGY Common from the middle tidal level, and is active in air.

DISTRIBUTION Widespread across the Atlantic, English Channel and North Sea.

Laver Spire Shell
Hydrobia ulvae

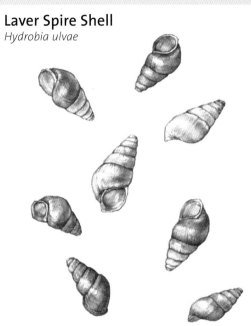

SIZE AND DESCRIPTION Height to 0.6cm. Small and thinly conical shell with six distinct narrow whorls. Apex is bluntly pointed. Shell is most commonly yellowish-brown, but variable.

HABITAT AND ECOLOGY Very abundant in salt marshes and estuarine mudflats, extending from the middle shore to more brackish waters. Grazes on Sea Lettuce (page 21).

DISTRIBUTION Widespread in the Atlantic, English Channel, North Sea and Baltic.

Tower Shell
Turritella communis

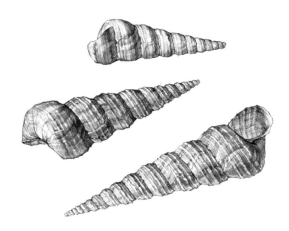

SIZE AND DESCRIPTION Height to 6cm. Distinctive long and tapering whorled shell. It is tall and thin, only about 1cm across, with up to 19 distinct whorls. Each lower whorl has three or so further ridges, and the aperture is rounded. Shell is variable in colour from near-white, through red, to brown.

HABITAT AND ECOLOGY Frequently abundant at some depth in muddy gravel beaches, but often washed up when empty.

DISTRIBUTION Common in the Atlantic, English Channel, North Sea and Mediterranean.

Pelican's Foot Shell
Aporrhais pespelecani

SIZE AND DESCRIPTION Height to 5cm. Resembles a tower shell except that the edges of the aperture are drawn out into four massive pointed fins. Has about nine well-marked whorls, each with a line of raised pointed knobs. In mature specimens the projections from the edge of the aperture are almost as long as the spire. Colour varies from pinkish- or yellowish-grey, to brown or even black.

HABITAT AND ECOLOGY A deep-water species not normally found living on the shore, although it is occasionally washed up and often dredged up.

DISTRIBUTION Common in the Atlantic, English Channel, North Sea and Mediterranean.

Slipper Limpet
Crepidula fornicata

SIZE AND DESCRIPTION Length to 5cm. Easily recognized slipper-shaped shell. It is roughly oval, and its resemblance to a slipper is enhanced by an interior ledge extending to half the length of the shell.

HABITAT AND ECOLOGY Tends to occur in chains, with the lowest individual attached to a rock or another mollusc, and subsequent individuals on the back of the first. The bottom animals are the oldest and female, while those higher up start as males, becoming females later. Empty shells and chains are frequently washed up.

DISTRIBUTION Originally an accidental introduction from America. Now very common around British waters.

European Cowrie
Trivia monacha

SIZE AND DESCRIPTION Length to 1cm. Typical cowrie, similar to the larger tropical forms, but much smaller. Oval, with a slit-like delicately ribbed opening along one side. Colour is variable, from cream to pink-orange or even brown above, usually paler below; there are generally three dark brown spots on the upper surface.

HABITAT AND ECOLOGY Occurs from the lower tidal level down to shallow water, usually among sea-squirts, on which it feeds.

DISTRIBUTION Found in the Atlantic, English Channel, North Sea and Mediterranean, though not generally commonly seen.

Common Wentletrap
Clathrus clathrus

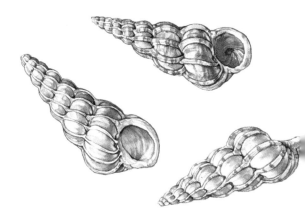

SIZE AND DESCRIPTION Height to 4cm, occasionally more. An elegant shell formed of a tall spire with up to 15 whorls, marked with prominent longitudinal ridges. These run along the length of the shell, crossing each suture at right angles. The mouth is circular. Colour varies from pale yellow to reddish-brown.

HABITAT AND ECOLOGY Rarely found living above low-tide level, but often washed up on shore. Occurs in deeper water, migrating to shallower areas at spawning time.

DISTRIBUTION Widespread in the Atlantic, English Channel, North Sea, Baltic and Mediterranean.

Violet Sea Snail
Ianthina exigua

Size and description Height to 1.7cm. Strikingly coloured whorled shell. It has a highly distinctive strong violet colour in life, but an empty shell fades gradually.

Habitat and ecology A pelagic species that floats on the surface using a mucus raft full of trapped air bubbles, feeding on free-floating colonial hydrozoans. Shells are occasionally washed up in large numbers after gales.

Distribution Common in the Atlantic.

Large Necklace Shell
Euspira catena

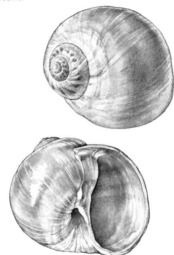

SIZE AND DESCRIPTION Height to 5cm. Large snail-like shell with a strong shine on the surface. It is 4–5cm wide with 6–7 whorls formed into a very short spire. Colour varies from yellow, through orange, to red, polished-looking and marked with red. Common Necklace Shell (*E. alderi*) is similar, but smaller and with rows of reddish-brown dots on the outside.

HABITAT AND ECOLOGY In life it burrows in the sand from the lower shore down, but it is frequently found washed up on sandy beaches.

DISTRIBUTION Locally common and widespread.

Dogwhelk
Nucella lapillus

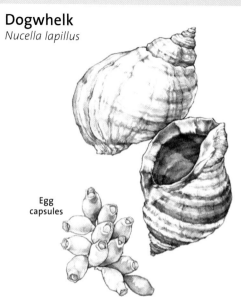

Egg capsules

Size and description Height to 4cm. Very common, heavily built snail-like shell with a short pointed spire. Colour is highly variable, from yellow-grey to white, sometimes brown and white striped. Colour varies according to diet, with the brown-striped version being most common where mussels are the main prey. Egg capsules are very distinctive, like masses of grains of brown rice standing on end.

Habitat and ecology Occurs from the middle and lower shores down to shallow water on rocky coasts, often in huge numbers. Predatory on barnacles, and less often on mussels.

Distribution Found in the Atlantic, English Channel and North Sea.

Sting Winkle
Ocenebra erinacea

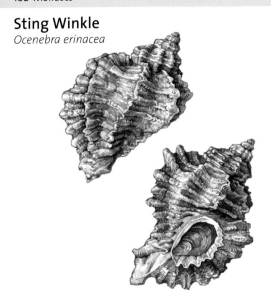

SIZE AND DESCRIPTION Height to 6cm. Similar in shape to Dogwhelk (page 101), but slightly larger and much more sculptured. Shell has 8–10 whorls and a well-marked spire. It is heavily ridged transversely, with a few ridges running at right angles. Also called Oyster Drill.

HABITAT AND ECOLOGY Locally common on rocky and gravelly shores from low water down, but coming further inshore to spawn in early summer. Predatory on shellfishes, especially oysters, and also barnacles, which it attacks by drilling through the shell.

DISTRIBUTION Occurs across the Atlantic, English Channel, North Sea and Mediterranean.

Common Whelk
Buccinum undatum

Egg capsules

SIZE AND DESCRIPTION Height to 10cm. Large and robust spiralled shell that is often found washed up empty. In deeper water individuals may grow to 15cm long. Shell has 7–8 ridged and sutured whorls. Empty shells often provide homes for hermit crabs. Egg capsules are also frequently washed up, and the bubbly spongy masses are almost as familiar as the shell.

HABITAT AND ECOLOGY Common in sandy and muddy gravel areas, living on the lower shore down, although empty shells may be found anywhere.

DISTRIBUTION Occurs in the Atlantic, English Channel, North Sea and western Baltic.

Netted Dogwhelk
Nassarius reticulatus

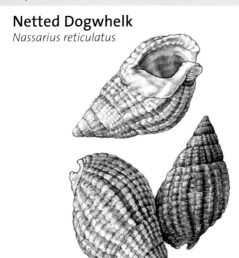

SIZE AND DESCRIPTION Height to 3.5cm. Attractively patterned delicate whelk with a conical spiral shell. Colour is pale to dark brown, and the shell is strongly marked with intersecting ridges producing a square pattern. Aperture is oval, with a markedly toothed outer lip. Thick-lipped Dogwhelk (*N. incrassatus*) is about half the size and found in rocky and less polluted waters.

HABITAT AND ECOLOGY Common on a variety of shore types, from the lower shore to deeper water, though it is often washed up empty. Lives by scavenging, unlike most other whelks, which are predatory.

DISTRIBUTION Occurs throughout the Atlantic, English Channel, North Sea, Baltic and Mediterranean.

Canoe Bubble
Scaphander lignarius

SIZE AND DESCRIPTION Length to 8cm. Resembles a blunt canoe or coracle, hence its name. Shell is usually yellowish-brown or creamy outside, and sometimes striped; inside is white. It is occupied by a white or pinkish animal that reaches 14–15cm in length and is unable to withdraw into the shell.

HABITAT AND ECOLOGY Inhabits shallow water below the low-water mark, on soft sandy or muddy substrates. Usually only the washed-up empty shells are found on beaches.

DISTRIBUTION Common in the Mediterranean, and northwards through the Atlantic as far as the English Channel.

Sea Lemon
Archidoris pseudoargus

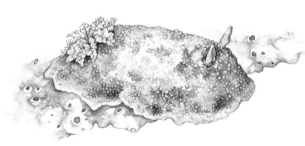

SIZE AND DESCRIPTION Length to 7cm. Resembles a large yellowish slug. Body is usually yellowish with brown, green or pink mottled blotches. There are two unbranched head tentacles, and a ring of nine large and much-branched pinkish gills at the rear end. This species does not have a shell. Various related species.

HABITAT AND ECOLOGY Common in shallow water, moving further up the shore from spring onwards to spawn, usually among rocks. Feeds on Breadcrumb Sponge (page 74).

DISTRIBUTION Occurs in the Atlantic, English Channel and North Sea.

Sea Hare
Aplysia punctata

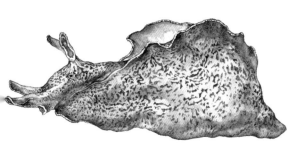

Size and description Length to 20cm. A strange creature that is
barely recognizable as having a shell. It is large and slug-like, with
four head tentacles, almost totally enclosing the thin, translucent
and oval pale brown shell. It varies in colour according to age and
conditions, from red to green. Similar but larger species inhabit
the Mediterranean.

Habitat and ecology Normally occurs offshore in kelp beds. In summer
comes closer inshore to spawn, depositing strings of pink or orange
eggs. Shell may be found washed up on shore.

Distribution Locally common in the Atlantic, English Channel and
North Sea.

Tusk Shell
Dentalium entalis

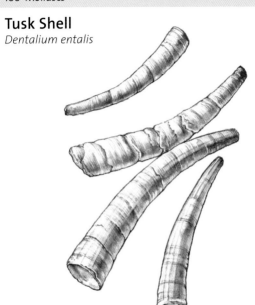

SIZE AND DESCRIPTION Length to 5cm. Species that most resembles a tiny elephant's tusk. The tapering hollow white shell is usually slightly curved. In life, a three-lobed foot projects from the wider end, which burrows into sand, while the narrower end emerges into the water.

HABITAT AND ECOLOGY Occurs in sand and mud in deeper water offshore only, but the shells are sufficiently resilient to withstand being washed up.

DISTRIBUTION Common in the Atlantic, English Channel and North Sea, and more frequent in the north.

Common Sea Slug
Aeolidia papillosa

SIZE AND DESCRIPTION Length to 8cm. Extraordinary-looking marine slug most notable for the dense covering of fine brownish or greenish appendages, which give the impression of fur, generally with a definite parting along the back. There are two distinct unbranched head tentacles.

HABITAT AND ECOLOGY Occurs throughout the intertidal area, mainly on rocky shores, particularly underneath rocks, where it is easily missed. Feeds on sea-anemones.

DISTRIBUTION Common in the Atlantic, English Channel and North Sea.

Noah's Ark
Arca noae

SIZE AND DESCRIPTION Length to 8cm. Large and rather shapeless and untidy bivalve shell. Valves may be found singly or attached together. Exterior is brown, uneven and often shaggy; interior is silvery. Hinge is long and straight with numerous small teeth.

HABITAT AND ECOLOGY Occurs firmly attached to rocks or stones by tiny threads (known as byssus) from the lowest shore downwards, although the empty shells may be washed up.

DISTRIBUTION Uncommon, and can be found only in the Atlantic and Mediterranean.

Dog Cockle
Glycymeris glycymeris

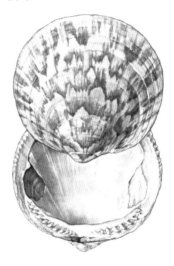

SIZE AND DESCRIPTION Length to 8cm. Large bivalve with an almost circular shell. Valves are pale yellow-brown marked with rows of reddish-brown zigzag markings, which look painted on. Markings may be lost in old or well-worn individuals. Interior is white. Also called Comb Shell.

HABITAT AND ECOLOGY Common offshore in muddy, sandy and gravelly water, and the empty shells are often washed up.

DISTRIBUTION Found across the Atlantic, English Channel, Baltic and Mediterranean.

Common Mussel
Mytilus edulis

SIZE AND DESCRIPTION Length to 15cm. Occurs in large masses and needs little description, though it is in fact highly variable. Colour varies from brown to purple and black, though blue-black is most common. Interior is pearly with a darker border.

HABITAT AND ECOLOGY Occurs abundantly on rocky, stony and even muddy shores, both on exposed coasts and in estuaries, often in very extensive beds.

DISTRIBUTION Found in the Atlantic, English Channel, North Sea, Baltic and Mediterranean.

Bearded Horse Mussel
Modiolus barbatus

SIZE AND DESCRIPTION Length to 6cm. Resembles a small whiskered version of Horse Mussel (page 114), and is of a similar shape. It has rows of whiskers towards the broader end of the shell, forming a shaggy 'fur'. Colour is brown-purple outside, paler silvery-blue inside.

HABITAT AND ECOLOGY Occurs on rocky and stony shores from the lowest shore down into deep water, among algae or around boulders.

DISTRIBUTION Widely distributed in the Atlantic, English Channel, North Sea and Mediterranean.

Horse Mussel
Modiolus modiolus

SIZE AND DESCRIPTION Length to 20cm; more commonly 12–15cm. Largest mussel in British waters. Both valves are similar. Shell is thick with a horny outer surface, or spiny in young individuals. It is purple or brown on the outside. Interior is silvery-blue and smooth. In life the animal is dark orange.

HABITAT AND ECOLOGY Common, though not in extensive beds, from the lower shore down to deep water. Particularly frequent among holdfasts of kelp. Empty shells are often washed up.

DISTRIBUTION Occurs in the Atlantic as far south as northern Spain, the English Channel and the North Sea. Most common in north of area.

Wing Oyster
Pteria hirundo

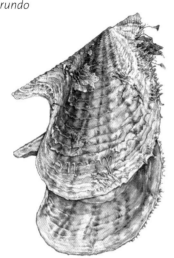

SIZE AND DESCRIPTION Length to 7.5cm. Looks unlike other mussels. The two valves are slightly different in shape, both being elongated into a fin-like structure, although one is larger than the other. Shell is silvery grey-brown outside, pearly white inside.

HABITAT AND ECOLOGY Occurs attached to stones in muddy, gravelly substrates from just below low water down to considerable depths, though shells are washed up occasionally.

DISTRIBUTION Common in the Atlantic south from Britain and in the English Channel.

Fan Mussel
Pinna fragilis

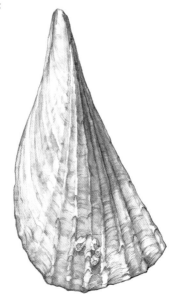

Size and description Length to 35cm. Distinctive bivalve resembling a folded fan, with a maximum width of about 25cm. Shape is triangular in outline and colour is usually brown, paler inside.
Habitat and ecology In life occurs in sand, gravel and mud, standing vertically with the point buried in the substrate, attached to a stone or other object by fine threads. The empty shells may be washed up.
Distribution Common across the Atlantic, mainly southern, and English Channel.

Common Oyster
Ostrea edulis

SIZE AND DESCRIPTION Length to 12cm. Well-known large shellfish with ridged circular valves and a 'mother-of-pearl' interior. Shell is variable in shape, but usually almost round and saucer-shaped, and brown in colour. Exterior of each valve bears a prominent sculpturing that aids recognition. Interior is smooth and pearly-white.

HABITAT AND ECOLOGY Very common in dense beds in estuaries or other muddy, gravelly or stony situations, and widely cultivated in commercial beds. Empty shells are washed ashore in large quantities.

DISTRIBUTION Occurs across the Atlantic, English Channel, North Sea and Mediterranean.

Portuguese Oyster
Crassostrea angulata

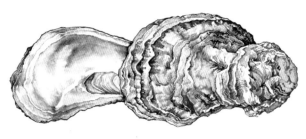

SIZE AND DESCRIPTION Length to 8cm; width to 18cm. Similar to Common Oyster (page 117), although more elongated and less circular, and larger and more irregular in shape. Valves are different from each other, with one being distinctly trough shaped, the other flatter. Upper surface is pale brown, deeply folded and sculptured; interior is smooth and white.

HABITAT AND ECOLOGY Imported into British waters from the Bay of Biscay, and now widespread and partially naturalized. Found in similar habitats to Common Oyster.

DISTRIBUTION Occurs in the Atlantic, English Channel and North Sea.

Great Scallop
Pecten maximus

SIZE AND DESCRIPTION Length to 15cm. Large bivalve with a typical scallop shape. The two valves are different, with the lower valve being rather saucer shaped, and the upper one flatter. They are reddish-brown with white markings. 'Ears' of the hinge are equal in size. Also called St James's Shell.

HABITAT AND ECOLOGY Common in sandy, gravelly and occasionally muddy areas, from shallow water down to very deep water. Often washed up.

DISTRIBUTION Found in the Atlantic, English Channel and North Sea.

Variegated Scallop
Chlamys varia

SIZE AND DESCRIPTION Length to 8cm. Medium-sized scallop. Valves are distinctly tapered towards the hinge, where one 'ear' is several times larger than the other. Colour is variable, most commonly purple, red, yellowish or brown, occasionally white, often patchily mottled. Surface is markedly ribbed, and the ribs may have small teeth. There are several similar species.

HABITAT AND ECOLOGY When alive occurs from the lowest shore level down to deep water, either free living or attached to the substrate by threads. Often washed up empty.

DISTRIBUTION Widely distributed and common in the Atlantic, English Channel, North Sea and Mediterranean.

Queen Scallop
Aequipecten opercularis

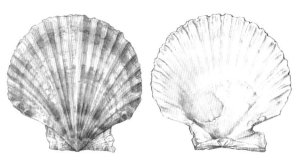

Size and description Length to 9cm. Larger than Variegated Scallop (opposite), with 'ears' more equal in size. Very variable in colour, which may be brown, red or yellow, frequently mottled or striped.
Habitat and ecology Adult is completely free swimming, moving around in large shoals over sandy or muddy sea floors by flapping its shells. When young it is attached to a stone or other solid object, but it becomes free later. Frequently washed up on beaches.
Distribution Common and widespread in the Atlantic, English Channel, North Sea and Mediterranean.

Tiger Scallop
Palliolum tigerinum

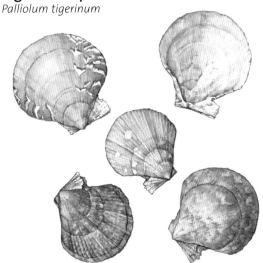

SIZE AND DESCRIPTION Length to 3cm. Relatively smooth scallop that is much smaller than the other scallops. External surface is usually smooth, although it may be finely ridged. Colour is variable, but generally somewhere between brown and white, often with stripes or blotches. The 'ears' are markedly uneven in size.

HABITAT AND ECOLOGY A free-swimming species, apart from in the early stages, although inactive and mainly found in crevices or under stones. Common offshore from extreme low water down to deep water. Empty shells are often washed up.

DISTRIBUTION Found in the Atlantic, English Channel and North Sea.

Common Saddle Oyster
Anomia ephippium

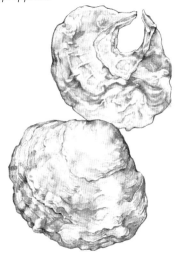

SIZE AND DESCRIPTION Length to 6cm. Large bivalve with distinctly different valves. The lower valve is flatter and thinner than the upper valve, and pierced by a hole through which the animal attaches itself to substrates, making the shell appear part of the rock. The other valve is larger, thicker and more dished. Ribbed Saddle Oyster (*Monia patelliformis*) is similar, but smaller and more ribbed.

HABITAT AND ECOLOGY Common from the middle shore down to deep water, attached to rocks or other hard substrates.

DISTRIBUTION Widespread in the Atlantic, English Channel, North Sea and Mediterranean.

Cockle-like Shell
Goodalia triangularis

SIZE AND DESCRIPTION Diameter to 4mm. Very small cockle-like shell that is most commonly white or yellowish. Both valves have a rounded triangular outline with a strongly marked umbo (hooked prominence at apex of each half of a bivalve mollusc's shell) and a yellowish-orange periostracum (thin layer of hardened protein on outer surface of shell).

HABITAT AND ECOLOGY Occurs offshore in muddy substrates to a considerable depth.

DISTRIBUTION Found across the Atlantic, English Channel, North Sea and Mediterranean.

Spiny Cockle
Acanthocardia aculeata

SIZE AND DESCRIPTION Length to 11cm. Impressive large plump cockle. Valves are very similar in size and shape, marked by 20 or so ribs running from the umbo to the edge and bearing sharp spines, which are distinctly separate from each other. Exterior is yellow-brown, inside pearly-white, with ridges still visible. Easily confused with Prickly Cockle (page 126).

HABITAT AND ECOLOGY Occurs in sandy areas offshore, from about 10m down to deep water. Empty shells are frequently washed up.

DISTRIBUTION Very widespread in the Atlantic, English Channel, North Sea, Baltic and Mediterranean.

Prickly Cockle
Acanthocardia tuberculata

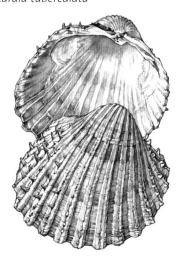

Size and description Length to 8cm. Very similar to Spiny Cockle (page 125), though generally slightly smaller. Distinguishable by the rather more rounded and bulkier shell, the stronger and larger spines, and the rounded tubercles over the lower part of the ribs.

Habitat and ecology Similar to that of Spiny Cockle. Found in sandy or muddy places offshore, from about 3m depth. Often washed up.

Distribution Occurs in the Atlantic, English Channel, North Sea and parts of the Baltic.

Common Cockle
Cerastoderma edule

SIZE AND DESCRIPTION Length to 5cm. Well-known and abundant species whose empty shells are often found, valves still joined, on sandy and muddy shores. Shell is pale yellowish-brown outside, marked with concentric brown lines, and almost white inside. Numerous ridges radiate out from the hinge, ending in undulations on the margin that are repeated inside the shell for a short distance.

HABITAT AND ECOLOGY One of the few properly intertidal cockles, occurring abundantly on the lower and middle shores, and down into shallow water, often in dense cockle beds.

DISTRIBUTION Widespread in the Atlantic, English Channel, North Sea and Mediterranean.

Warty Venus
Venus verrucosa

SIZE AND DESCRIPTION Length to 7cm. Large and solid cockle-like bivalve. Valves are brownish, yellowish or grey outside, white inside. There are strongly marked concentric ridges right across the shell that break up into teeth or tubercles towards the edge, and three cardinal teeth on each valve at the hinge. Similar species include the smaller and more finely ridged Striped Venus (*V. striatula*) and Banded Venus (*V. fasciata*), which is very small (2–3cm long) and has strongly marked ridges.

HABITAT AND ECOLOGY Common in sandy or gravelly areas from low tide down to deep water.

DISTRIBUTION Widespread throughout the Atlantic, English Channel and Mediterranean.

Pullet Carpet Shell
Venerupis pullastra

SIZE AND DESCRIPTION Length to 5cm. Oval-shaped bivalve with markings resembling the plumage of a hen. Shell is about 3cm wide, and the valves are similarly shaped. It is golden-brown, attractively marked with lines running in two directions. Inside is pearly-white or silvery. Banded Carpet Shell (*V. rhomboides*) is similar with zigzag colour banding on the shell.

HABITAT AND ECOLOGY Very common from the lower shore down to deep water. Sometimes loosely attached by byssus threads (strong silky fibres made from protein) in sandy, gravelly and stony situations.

DISTRIBUTION Widespread in the Atlantic, English Channel, North Sea and Mediterranean.

Rayed Trough Shell
Mactra corallina

SIZE AND DESCRIPTION Length to 5cm. Medium to large, but rather thin and noticeably brittle bivalve. Both valves are similar in shape, like a rounded triangle. Distinct brownish and paler rays run from the umbo to the margin, crossing fine concentric ridges. Interior is pearly-white, sometimes pinky-purple.

HABITAT AND ECOLOGY Burrows in sandy or gravelly substrates from extreme low water down to deep water. Often washed up empty.

DISTRIBUTION Common and widespread in the Atlantic, English Channel, North Sea and Mediterranean.

Thick Trough Shell
Spisula solida

Size and description Length to 5cm. Very similar in shape to Rayed Trough Shell (opposite), but more solid for its size. Valves are pale and lack the brown rays running across the shell. When looked at closely it can be seen that this species has finely ridged cardinal teeth on the hinge, whereas those of the previous species are smooth.

Habitat and ecology As for Rayed Trough Shell.

Distribution Common and widespread in the Atlantic, English Channel and North Sea.

Common Otter Shell
Lutraria lutraria

SIZE AND DESCRIPTION Length to 14cm; more commonly 11–12cm. Familiar large oval shell typically covered with a peeling transparent sheath. Exterior is yellowish or brownish, and the sheath is often brown. Interior is pearly-white. Sand Gaper (*Mya arenaria*) is similar, but narrower and smaller overall.

HABITAT AND ECOLOGY Lives buried in sand or sandy mud from the lower shore down to deep water. Very often washed up when empty.

DISTRIBUTION Common and widespread in the Atlantic, English Channel and North Sea.

Blunt Tellin
Tellina crassa

SIZE AND DESCRIPTION Length to 6cm. Solid and rather plump bivalve with an undistinguished circular-triangular shape. One valve is slightly flatter than the other. Shell is yellowish or pale brown outside; interior is yellow-orange in the centre, white on the margin. There are numerous concentric ridges around the shell. Several similar species, which are not very easy to distinguish.

HABITAT AND ECOLOGY Lives buried in muddy sand and gravel, using its two siphons to feed with. Frequently washed up, with valves separate or joined.

DISTRIBUTION Locally common in the Atlantic, English Channel and North Sea.

Baltic Tellin
Macoma balthica

SIZE AND DESCRIPTION Length to 3cm. Similar to Blunt Tellin (page 133), but much smaller and usually more strongly coloured. One side of each valve is noticeably more pointed than the other. Colour is very variable, usually yellow-grey-white, but often banded with red, orange, darker grey or purple. Interior may be very pale through to purple, sometimes banded.

HABITAT AND ECOLOGY Very common in sand and mud just offshore in estuaries. Able to tolerate relatively low salinity (hence its abundance in the Baltic). Frequently washed up empty.

DISTRIBUTION Occurs in northern parts of the Atlantic, English Channel, North Sea and Baltic.

Large Sunset Shell
Gari depressa

SIZE AND DESCRIPTION Length to 6cm. Oval compressed bivalve similar to a small Common Otter Shell (page 132) in shape. Valves are compressed, both similar, and with a definite gap at the back where they meet. Colour is variable, usually pale pinky-brown with darker rays extending from the umbo to the edge. The peeling periostracum is greenish-brown, the interior pinky-white. Faroe Sunset Shell (*G. fervensis*) is smaller and mainly northern.

HABITAT AND ECOLOGY Occurs in sandy bottoms from extreme low water down to deep water. Often washed up, usually as single valves.

DISTRIBUTION Common throughout the Atlantic, English Channel, North Sea and Mediterranean.

Peppery Furrow Shell
Scrobicularia plana

SIZE AND DESCRIPTION Length to 6cm. Medium to large bivalve with attractive dark markings. Valves are similar, like rounded triangles in outline. Exterior is pale greyish-yellow, often marked with a few fine darker concentric lines, though often much of the broadest part is dark. Interior is silvery-white.

HABITAT AND ECOLOGY Lives buried in sandy or muddy areas from the upper beach down to shallow water. Very common in estuaries, and able to tolerate low salinities. Commonly washed up empty.

DISTRIBUTION Widespread in the Atlantic, English Channel, North Sea, Baltic and Mediterranean.

Pod Razor Shell
Ensis siliqua

Size and description Length to 20cm. Common and familiar species, and the largest of the razor shells, so-called due to its resemblance to an old-fashioned razor. The long and narrow valves are very similar in shape, with parallel sides. Colour is off-white with brown markings; conspicuous glossy brown-green periostracum. Exterior is marked with fine vertical and horizontal lines.

Habitat and ecology Lives buried in sand from the extreme lower shore down to deep water. Single or double valves are often washed up.

Distribution Common throughout the Atlantic, English Channel, North Sea and Mediterranean.

Curved Razor Shell
Ensis ensis

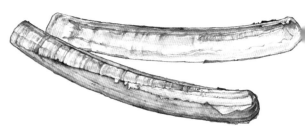

SIZE AND DESCRIPTION Length to 13cm. Smaller and more noticeably curved than Pod Razor Shell (page 137). Both margins of the valves are curved, and are roughly parallel with each other. Colour similar to that of Pod Razor. *E. arcuata*, a similar common and widespread razor shell, is almost as large as Pod Razor, but curved on one side and straight on the other.

HABITAT AND ECOLOGY Occurs in sand on the extreme lower shore.

DISTRIBUTION Found throughout the Atlantic, English Channel, North Sea and Mediterranean.

Blunt Gaper
Mya truncata

SIZE AND DESCRIPTION Length to 8cm. Gapers are rather like tellins and otter shells in shape, although this species is distinctive in having one end curved and the other blunt. Shell is broadly oval, with a marked gape at one end through which the siphon of the shell projects. Exterior is creamy-white to yellow; interior is pearly-white.

HABITAT AND ECOLOGY Commonly buried in sand and mud from the middle shore down to deep water.

DISTRIBUTION Widespread throughout the Atlantic, English Channel and North Sea.

Sand Gaper
Mya arenaria

SIZE AND DESCRIPTION Length to 14cm. Very similar to Blunt Gaper (page 139), but generally larger and more oval, without the blunt end.
HABITAT AND ECOLOGY Occurs in similar habitats to Blunt Gaper, in sand and mud, though found further up the shore, and is more common generally. Able to tolerate relatively lower salinities, and may be found in estuaries
DISTRIBUTION Widespread in the Atlantic, English Channel, North Sea and Baltic.

Common Piddock
Pholas dactylus

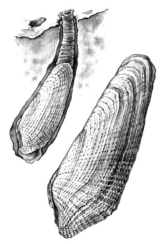

SIZE AND DESCRIPTION Length to 15cm. One of a small group of molluscs that are capable of burrowing into solid rock. Delicately ridged shell is only about 5cm wide and has a characteristic shape, with a distinct projection at one end and a wide gape. The similar Flask Shell (*Gastrochaena dubia*) is much smaller.

HABITAT AND ECOLOGY Occurs from the lower shore down to shallow water. Usually found boring into rock or wood, although also occurs in softer substrates. May be found washed up when its substrate has eroded.

DISTRIBUTION Found in the Atlantic from south-west Britain southwards, the English Channel and the Mediterranean.

Pandora Shell
Pandora albida

SIZE AND DESCRIPTION Length to 4cm. Distinctive rather delicate bivalve with a crescent-shaped shell. Finely ridged exterior is white, and often partly covered by the brown periostracum; interior is pearly-white. Valves are dissimilar, with the left valve being concave and trough-like, the right valve flatter and overlapping the left.

HABITAT AND ECOLOGY Occurs in sandy or muddy substrates, from low tide downwards, living on top of the sand rather than buried in it. Prefers sheltered conditions.

DISTRIBUTION Rather local and mainly southern, in the Atlantic, English Channel and North Sea.

Cuttlefish
Sepia officinalis

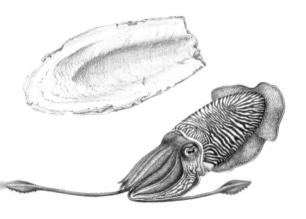

SIZE AND DESCRIPTION Length to 40cm. The 'cuttle bone' of this species is very well known, but the animal itself is rarely seen. It is rather flattened, with ten tentacles around the mouth, two of which are much longer than the rest. Shell is internal, and is often seen washed up. Similar species include the smaller and squatter Little Cuttle (*Sepiola atlantica*).

HABITAT AND ECOLOGY Lives close inshore. Sometimes found in pools or among eelgrass on the lower shore, particularly during the summer spawning season.

DISTRIBUTION Common in the Atlantic, English Channel, North Sea and Mediterranean, although rarer towards the north.

Great Shipworm
Teredo navalis

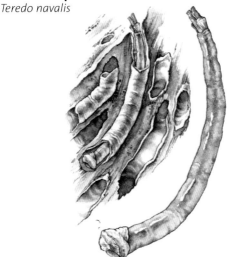

SIZE AND DESCRIPTION Length to 20cm. One of a distinctive group of shells. Its shell is greatly reduced and functions as a drill, enclosing only part of the animal. Most visible portion is the calcareous white tube secreted by the animal. It can be closed off by a pair of hard shutters (pallets) for protection when the mollusc is not feeding. Similar species include Large Shipworm (*T. norvegica*), which is often twice as large, and *T. megotara*, usually found in floating timber.

HABITAT AND ECOLOGY Lives in the wood of ships and harbours, using its shell as a drill.

DISTRIBUTION Common throughout the Atlantic, English Channel, North Sea and Baltic.

Goose Barnacle
Lepas anatifera

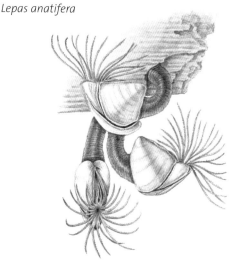

SIZE AND DESCRIPTION Length to 5cm. A strange species that attaches itself by a flexible stalk to floating wood. Shell is made up of five blue-tinged translucent plates, from which the animal projects to feed at one end. This part is attached to floating wood via a long brown stalk that can be partially retracted. Buoy-making Barnacle (*L. fascicularis*) is similar but smaller, and lives attached to its own spongy white float.

HABITAT AND ECOLOGY Normally pelagic, floating at sea, but often found washed up.

DISTRIBUTION Widespread throughout the Atlantic, English Channel and North Sea.

Acorn Barnacle
Semibalanus balanoides

SIZE AND DESCRIPTION Diameter to 10mm, rarely 15mm. Very variable in shape: tall and tubular when crowded, low and conical when solitary. Outline is round to oval with irregular margins. Shell is made up of six white, cream or greyish-brown plates.

HABITAT AND ECOLOGY Found attached to rocks, boulders, shells and artificial structures, typically on the lower shore

DISTRIBUTION Common and abundant on coasts from Arctic Norway to Spain.

Sea Slater
Ligia oceanica

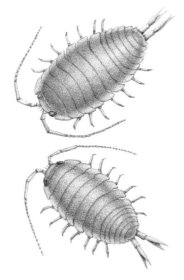

SIZE AND DESCRIPTION Length to 3cm. Like a large woodlouse. It has seven pairs of legs (six in female) and two large antennae, and is grey or slightly greenish-grey in colour, with dots. A very active species, especially at night, it is also fast moving if disturbed during the day.

HABITAT AND ECOLOGY Lives on the upper shore, particularly on rocks and near harbours, hiding under stones or in crevices.

DISTRIBUTION Widely distributed and common around the Atlantic, English Channel, North Sea and Mediterranean.

Sand hopper
Talitrus saltator

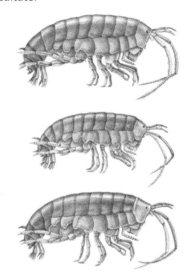

SIZE AND DESCRIPTION Length to 2.5cm. One of several jumping shrimp-like animals that live among rotting vegetation at the strand line. The slightly curved body is brownish, grey or greenish, with a black line along the back. Able to jump readily, unlike some related species; masses spring in all directions if disturbed.

HABITAT AND ECOLOGY Very common among rotting seaweed and under debris on sand, on the upper shore.

DISTRIBUTION Widespread around the coasts of the North Sea and north-east Atlantic from southern Norway to the Mediterranean.

Common Prawn
Leander serratus

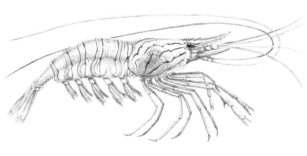

SIZE AND DESCRIPTION Length usually 5–7cm; sometimes to 10cm. Similar in appearance to other prawns. Body is transparent greyish with coloured dots and lines visible inside. Antennae are generally very long, and at least one is considerably longer than the body length. Many very similar species.

HABITAT AND ECOLOGY Occurs in rock pools on the lower shore down to shallow water. Particularly common in areas with algae in August–September, varying from year to year.

DISTRIBUTION Found across the Atlantic, English Channel and Mediterranean.

Common Shrimp
Crangon crangon

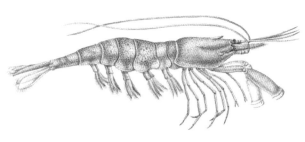

SIZE AND DESCRIPTION Length to 7cm. Similar and closely related to Common Prawn (page 149), although generally smaller and more slender. Greyish or brownish in colour. Longest antenna is as long as the body. Many very similar species.

HABITAT AND ECOLOGY Very common in shallow water, but particularly associated with sandy situations, unlike prawns. May be abundant in estuaries.

DISTRIBUTION Widespread throughout the North Sea and Baltic, south to the Mediterranean.

Common Lobster
Hommarus gammarus

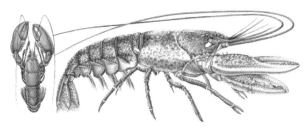

SIZE AND DESCRIPTION Length to 45cm; occasionally much longer. Very familiar sea animal, though unfortunately usually only seen when dead (above left). In life the body is basically blue, with small amounts of orange showing through. Similar species include Crawfish (*Palinurus vulgaris*), which lacks the large claws and is covered in spines.

HABITAT AND ECOLOGY Locally common in clean-water rocky areas, from the lowest tide mark down to deep water, usually under rocks or in cavities. Aggressive and solitary; the massive pincers can inflict a painful bite.

DISTRIBUTION Widespread from the Lofoten Islands in northern Norway to the western Baltic, Atlantic, English Channel, North Sea and Mediterranean coasts of Europe, south to north-west Africa and east to the Baltic Sea.

Squat Lobster
Galathea strigosa

SIZE AND DESCRIPTION Length to 15cm. Strange-looking creature that is most closely related to hermit crabs. Squat body is red with variable blue lines. Large pincers and main three pairs of legs are spiny and brownish in colour.

HABITAT AND ECOLOGY Widespread but not locally common on the lower shore down to deeper water. Can be very aggressive if threatened.

DISTRIBUTION Occurs across the Atlantic, English Channel, North Sea and Mediterranean.

Broad-clawed Porcelain Crab
Porcellana platycheles

SIZE AND DESCRIPTION Length to 3cm. Small roundish crab that is slightly longer than broad and appears to have only three pairs of legs, the fourth pair being small and folded under the tail. Overall colour is a rather muddy grey-brown, sometimes reddish. Large and broad pincers are hairy on the outer edges, as are the legs. Long-clawed Porcelain Crab (*P. longicornis*) is similar, but not hairy and with narrower claws and a round carapace.

HABITAT AND ECOLOGY Widely distributed and common in rocky and stony areas, on the middle and lower shores, often occurring underneath stones.

DISTRIBUTION Occurs across the Atlantic, English Channel, North Sea and Mediterranean.

Spider Crab
Macropodia tenuirostris

SIZE AND DESCRIPTION Length to 2cm (carapace). Animal that appears to be midway between a spider and a crab, although in fact it is a true crab. Carapace is roughly triangular, and dwarfed by the four pairs of long thin legs and two large pincers. Colour is yellowish-orange, though often masked by encrusting growths of algae and sponges.

HABITAT AND ECOLOGY Lives from the lowest shore level downwards, under stones or among seaweeds.

DISTRIBUTION Widely distributed in the Atlantic, English Channel, North Sea and Baltic.

Common Hermit Crab
Pagurus bernhardus

SIZE AND DESCRIPTION Length to 10cm, occasionally larger. Common seashore animal well known for its habit of occupying shells. The animal itself is rarely fully seen. Pincers are large and coarsely granulated, with the right pincer being much larger than the left.

HABITAT AND ECOLOGY Very common from the lower shore down to deeper water. Often associated with other animals such as Sulphur Sponges (page 73), parasitic barnacles and the sea-anemone *Calliactis parasitica*.

DISTRIBUTION Widely distributed on coasts in Iceland, Norway and the western Baltic, southwards to the North Sea, English Channel and Atlantic as far as Portugal.

Edible Crab
Cancer pagurus

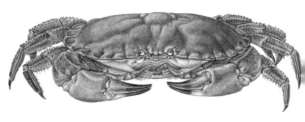

Size and description Length to 25cm, usually smaller (carapace). Large
or very large crab with heavy dark-tipped pincers. Overall colour is
brick-pink. Edge of the carapace is crimped into a series of lobes,
about ten on each side. Walking legs are hairy and rounded in section,
rather than flattened.

Habitat and ecology Common on the middle and lower shores,
especially where there are rocks, and down to deep water. Largest
individuals usually live well offshore.

Distribution Widespread in the Atlantic, English Channel, North Sea
and Mediterranean.

Masked Crab
Corystes cassivelaunus

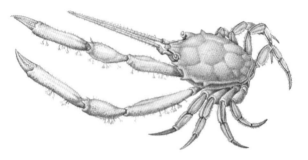

Size and description Length to 4cm; width to 3cm (carapace). Species notable for its long antennae. Body is pale brownish-yellow. Pincer claws are much longer than the body, and the exceptionally long and hairy antennae are joined together along their entire length, therefore tending to project directly forwards.

Habitat and ecology Widely distributed and not uncommon on the lower parts of sandy shores and into shallow water. Usually buried in the sand, where it can use its antennae to aid the passage of water to the gills.

Distribution Occurs across the Atlantic, English Channel, North Sea and Mediterranean.

Common Shore Crab

Carcinus maenas

SIZE AND DESCRIPTION Length to 8cm (carapace). Common small- to medium-sized crab. Carapace is brown or green (white or speckled in juveniles), and there are five sharp teeth on either side of the eyes. Undersurface is usually yellowish-green, the legs sometimes green or brick-red.

HABITAT AND ECOLOGY Very common on the middle and lower levels of all kinds of beaches, even in estuaries, and down to shallow water.

DISTRIBUTION Widespread on all European coasts.

Springtail
Lipura maritima

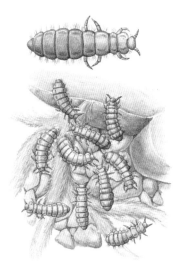

SIZE AND DESCRIPTION Length to 0.3cm. Body is narrow, and dark slaty-blue or grey in colour. There are three pairs of legs and a single pair of anntenae.

HABITAT AND ECOLOGY Occurs floating on the surfaces of rock pools on the upper shore, or occasionally crawling over rocks. Although individually very small, these little springtails become conspicuous because they live in dense groups.

DISTRIBUTION Widespread and common in the Atlantic, English Channel, North Sea and Mediterranean areas.

Bristle-tail
Petrobius maritimus

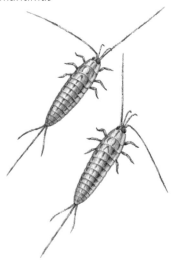

Size and description Length to 1.25cm. Close relative of the Silverfish, and similar in appearance to it. Antennae are very conspicuous, and are about as long as the silvery-grey body. Abdomen ends in three 'tails', of which the middle one is the longest. There are three pairs of legs, but no wings.

Habitat and ecology Common on the upper shore and above, living in crevices and under rocks, where it scavenges. Can move fast if the need arises.

Distribution Widespread on the Atlantic, English Channel, North Sea and Mediterranean coasts.

Sea-spider
Nymphon gracile

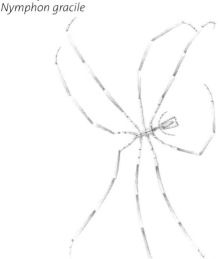

SIZE AND DESCRIPTION Length to 1cm (body). Extraordinary animal with a striking resemblance to a terrestrial spider. Body is so slender that it is not adequate to contain the animal's stomach, which extends up the legs. There are four main pairs of legs (plus a fifth, much-reduced pair), the longest of which is about 2.5cm. Colour is red or pinkish. Several other sea-spider species occur.

HABITAT AND ECOLOGY Reasonably common on the middle and lower shores, under stones and algae, and into shallow water.

DISTRIBUTION Occurs across the Atlantic, English Channel, North Sea and Mediterranean.

Common Starfish
Asterias rubens

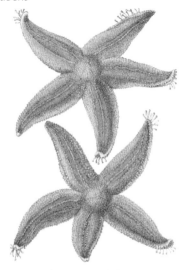

SIZE AND DESCRIPTION Length to 15cm; rarely larger, to 50cm. Five-pointed star-like animal that varies widely in size according to its age and situation. It has five regular arms, or points, which turn up at the ends when active, and is reddish, pink or orange above, paler below. Upper surface is covered by numerous small spines and tubercules. Several other species occur.

HABITAT AND ECOLOGY Common and widespread on lower shores, among rocks, in shellfish beds or among algae, down to deep water.

DISTRIBUTION Found in the Atlantic, English Channel, North Sea and western Baltic.

Spiny Starfish
Marthasterias glacialis

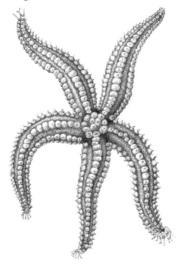

SIZE AND DESCRIPTION Length to 30cm; to 75cm in deeper water. Animal with the typical starfish shape, but covered all over the upper surface with large spines. Usually greenish, or yellowish to reddish, pale and well camouflaged. There are five arms, which taper gradually towards the ends; these may break off if the animal is picked up.

HABITAT AND ECOLOGY Moderately common, although rarely abundant, on lower shores, particularly where it is rocky or stony.

DISTRIBUTION Occurs in the Atlantic, western part of the English Channel, North Sea and Mediterranean.

Feather Star
Antedon bifida

SIZE AND DESCRIPTION Length to 15cm (arm). Plant-like animal consisting of a small disc with five pairs of long and feathery arms. Disc attaches temporarily to stones and rocks, and the arms wave about in the water. Colour is usually some shade of red, pink or purple, occasionally yellowish, and the arms may be striped.

HABITAT AND ECOLOGY Widespread but very local from the extreme lowest shore downwards, among rocks and stones.

DISTRIBUTION Occurs in the Atlantic, English Channel and northern part of North Sea.

Common Brittle Star
Ophiothrix fragilis

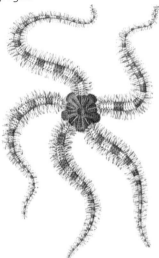

Size and description Length to 10cm (arm). One of a distinctive group of animals consisting of a tiny central disc, about 2cm in diameter, with five long radiating arms. Colour is very variable, but usually bright red, purple, orange or violet, often strongly patterned or striped on the upper surface. Very fragile. One of the most common of the group, members of which are difficult to distinguish from each other.

Habitat and ecology Common and widespread on the lower shore and into deep water, among stones, rocks and algae.

Distribution Occurs across the Atlantic, English Channel, North Sea and Mediterranean.

Edible Sea-urchin
Echinus esculentus

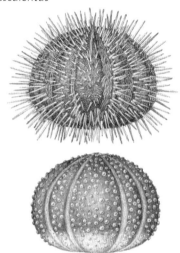

SIZE AND DESCRIPTION Diameter to 10cm; may reach 17cm. Familiar animal both in its fully spined living form, and as a spineless empty 'test', or shell-like case. The test is an almost spherical ball that is slightly flattened at each 'pole'. Spines are reddish-pink, and often tipped with purple. Test itself is red, orange or purple, with white scars from spines clearly visible. Several other species.

HABITAT AND ECOLOGY Common and widespread, particularly in early summer, from the extreme lower shore down to deep water, among rocks, stones and algae.

DISTRIBUTION Occurs in the Atlantic, English Channel and North Sea.

Mermaid's Purse
Scyliorhinus canicula

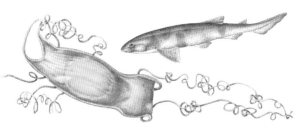

SIZE AND DESCRIPTION Length to 6cm (excluding tendrils). Well known to beachcombers, these capsules are the empty egg cases of the Lesser-spotted Dogfish, or Smooth Hound. They are laid offshore, attached to algae or other substrate by long twisted tendrils. The embryonic fish has usually hatched by the time the case is washed up. Each capsule is brownish in colour, fading later. Egg capsule of Greater Spotted Dogfish (*S. stellaris*) is about twice as large. Egg capsules of skates and rays have points or horns rather than tendrils, although they are otherwise similar. All are widespread and may be found almost anywhere on the shore.

Rock Goby
Gobius paganellus

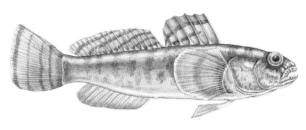

Size and description Length to 12cm. Head is large and the body is thickset. Eyes are on top of the head, the mouth is thick-lipped and the cheeks are large. Front dorsal (back) fin has an orange band. General colour is dull brownish or dark grey. One of many similar gobies, including the spotted Leopard Goby (*Thorogobius ephippiatus*).

Habitat and ecology Widespread and common in rock pools and among algae on the lower shore.

Distribution Occurs throughout the Atlantic, English Channel and Mediterranean.

Worm Pipefish
Nerophis lumbriciformis

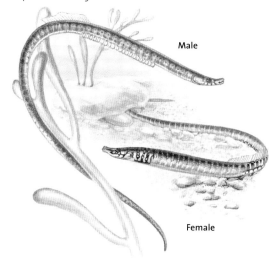

Male

Female

SIZE AND DESCRIPTION Length to 17cm. Very elongated and slender pipe-like fish. Head is small with a short snout that turns upwards. Single small dorsal fin. Body dark brown to olive, sometimes with pale spots or stripes. Pipefish are closely related to seahorses.

HABITAT AND ECOLOGY Occurs among algae in rocky areas on the shore down to 30m. Female lays eggs in a groove on male's belly. Male guards the eggs and young until they grow to about 1cm long. Diet comprises small crustaceans.

DISTRIBUTION Found from southern Norway to Morocco. Common on most British and Irish coasts; rare on east coast of Britain.

Shanny
Lipophrys pholis

SIZE AND DESCRIPTION Length to 16cm. Relatively large and blunt face, and thickset tapering body with a dorsal fin along the length of the back. Eyes are located on top of the head, and mouth is large with thick lips.

HABITAT AND ECOLOGY Occurs on rocky coastlines and sandy shores, in intertidal and subtidal zones down to about 30m. Eggs are laid under stones and guarded by male. Feeds on small fish, algae, barnacles and mussels.

DISTRIBUTION Found from southern Norway to Morocco, but not in Mediterranean. Very common around coasts of Britain and Ireland.

Tompot Blenny
Parablennius gattorugine

SIZE AND DESCRIPTION Length to 30cm. Stoutly built blenny with an elongated body and relatively large head with two distinctive branched head tentacles above the eyes. Long dorsal fin is separated into two by a shallow notch. Pectoral fins are large and rounded, and there is a single long anal fin. Colour is mottled brown with vertical darker bars running across the sides.

HABITAT AND ECOLOGY Occurs intertidally in rock pools or subtidally down to 20m, in holes, on rocky ledges and among boulders and algae. Female lays eggs in a hole or crevice, and male guards them until they are hatched. Feeds mainly on crustaceans.

DISTRIBUTION Found from west coast of Britain and all around Ireland, to Mediterranean and Adriatic.

Pogge
Agonus cataphractus

SIZE AND DESCRIPTION Length to 15cm. Distinctive fish in which the body surface is encased in protective overlapping bony plates. There is a strong spine on each gill cover and a pair of hooked spines on the snout. Numerous short barbels on the underside of the head help the fish locate prey. Usually mottled dark greyish-brown; underside is creamy-white. Also called Armed Bullhead.

HABITAT AND ECOLOGY Lives in sandy and muddy sea beds, from shallow water down to 500m. May occur in estuaries. Feeds on small crustaceans and other bottom-living invertebrates.

DISTRIBUTION Found in the Atlantic, English Channel, North Sea and western Baltic, although uncommon.

Sea Scorpion
Taurulus bubalis

SIZE AND DESCRIPTION Length to 17cm. Small fish with a stout body, large head with eyes positioned on top, distinctive barbel at the corners of the mouth and long spine in front of the gill cover. Pectoral fins are large in relation to its body. Colour is variable, matching surroundings, usually brownish mottled with cream, or orange or red with pale blotches in some areas.

HABITAT AND ECOLOGY Common in rock pools and under algae on the lower shore, and sublittorally in algae-covered rock to 30m. Feeds on crustaceans and small bottom-living fish.

DISTRIBUTION Occurs from northern Scandinavia to north-western Mediterranean, including southern Baltic. Common around coasts of Britain and Ireland.

Lumpsucker
Cyclopterus lumpus

SIZE AND DESCRIPTION Length to 50cm (female). Massive stout body with a bony head and four rows of bony plates and tubercles. Modified pelvic fins have evolved into adhesive discs (as in the sea snails, *Liparis*), which the fish use to adhere to the substrate. Female about twice the size of male. In breeding season male turns from drab greyish-green to bright red or orange.

HABITAT AND ECOLOGY Lives on sea bottom, hiding in crevices between rocks and under stones, and migrates from deeper waters to shallow waters to spawn in spring. Female lays about 200,000 yellowish eggs among rocks at low-tide level, where they are guarded by male. Diet includes small crustaceans and jellyfishes.

DISTRIBUTION Common in the Atlantic south to Portugal.

Corkwing Wrasse
Crenilabrus melops

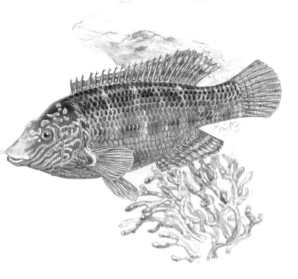

SIZE AND DESCRIPTION Length to 20cm. Laterally flattened body with a relatively small head, a large mouth with thick lips and a single long dorsal fin. Colouration variable, from green and greenish-brown, to green or reddish; often a dark spot in the tail-base centre. Male has blue-green wavy or curved lines on his head.

HABITAT AND ECOLOGY Subtidal over algae-covered rocks at 1–30m, and found in rock pools. Young wrasse often occur in eelgrass beds.

DISTRIBUTION Common on coasts of the Atlantic, North Sea, southern Baltic and western Mediterranean, except far north.

Butterfish
Pholis gunnellus

SIZE AND DESCRIPTION Length to 25cm. Long and slender bronze-, reddish- to pinkish-brown fish with 12 or more light-ringed dark spots along the back. Head and mouth are very small, and there is a single dorsal fin from behind the head to the tail fin. Anal fin is present from about halfway along the body to the tail fin.

HABITAT AND ECOLOGY Common on rocky shores in rock pools, under rocks or among seaweed. Occurs subtidally down to 100m in rocky areas, and also in other habitats. Lays eggs in a clump among rocks, or in shells or burrows of other animals; eggs are guarded by both parents. Feeds on various small invertebrates such as crustaceans and molluscs.

DISTRIBUTION Found from Iceland to the Bay of Biscay. Common around all coasts of Britain and Ireland.

Fifteen-spined Stickleback
Spinachia spinachia

Size and description Length to 22cm. Elongated slender fish with triangular-shaped dorsal and anal fins, and 14–17 short spines along the back. Greenish-brown to dark brown on upper side and sides, and paler on underside.

Habitat and ecology Intertidal in rock pools, and subtidal down to 10m. Lives in algae and seagrasses. Male builds a nest from algae held together by shiny secretional threads (tangspiggin) in spring to early summer. Eggs are laid in nest and guarded by male until they hatch. Diet comprises small invertebrates.

Distribution Found from northern Norway to Atlantic coasts of France, and inhabits all coasts of Britain and Ireland.

Two-spotted Clingfish
Diplecogaster bimaculata

SIZE AND DESCRIPTION Length to 4cm. Fish with a sucker under the front end of its body that allows it to cling to rocks. Head is wider than the rest of the body, which is laterally compressed. Usually reddish-brown, or red with patches along the back, and a paler ventral surface that is sometimes yellowish. Two blue spots on the back of the head.

HABITAT AND ECOLOGY Lives intertidally on the lower shore in rock pools and under rocks. Individuals may guard eggs under rocks.

DISTRIBUTION Found from Norway to the Mediterranean. In Britain occurs around the south-west and west coasts, and all around Ireland.

Montagu's Sea Snail
Liparis montagui

SIZE AND DESCRIPTION Length to 10cm. Small fish with a tadpole-shaped body and a relatively large head. A sucker on the underside formed from the pelvic fins enables it to grip rocks. Skin is scaleless and smooth looking. Colour is variable, ranging from brown or yellow, to red or green.

HABITAT AND ECOLOGY Found on rocky shores down to 30m, clinging to undersides of rocks or onto algae. Breeds early in the year, and lays eggs on algae. Feeds on small crustaceans.

DISTRIBUTION Occurs from northern Norway and Iceland to the Bay of Biscay. Common around coasts of Britain and Ireland, though rare in south-east Britain.

Birds of the Seashore

Certain birds visit coasts to feed on the rich bounty of marine life found here, with the species usually varying from season to season. A small selection of birds that might be seen on the seashore is featured on the following pages.

Brent Goose (*Branta bernicla*) Small black goose that spends the winter on British coasts. Feeds on intertidal eelgrass and other vegetation. Light-bellied race (*B. b. hrota*) occurs on the west coast of Britain and in Ireland, Dark-bellied (*B. b. bernicla*) in the east and south.

Dark-bellied race

Light-bellied race

Shelduck (*Tadorna tadorna*) Inhabits estuaries, sandy shores and salt marshes. Breeds mainly on coasts. Feeds chiefly on tiny molluscs like Laver Spire Shells (page 93), which are caught by sweeping with a side-to-side beak movement of the flattened bill.

Juvenile

Female

Male

Young male

Female

Male

Common Eider (*Somateria mollissima*) Found on the sea and in rocky coastal areas. More common in north and Scotland and Ireland, where it breeds, than in southern Britain. Dives for crustaceans and molluscs.

Cormorant (*Phalacrocorax carbo*) Present all year on coasts. Nests in colonies, usually on rocks on coasts. On land displays characteristic 'heraldic' pose with wings held out; swims low in the water. Feeds almost exclusively on fishes, catching them by diving.

Breeding plumage

Grey Heron (*Ardea cinerea*) Common year round in all kinds of habitats near water, including the seashore. Nests in colonies, usually in tall trees, in huge nests. Feeds on fishes, amphibians, small mammals, insects and reptiles.

Bill Adaptations

Many wading birds have specially adapted bills that help them extract food from sand or mud. Plovers (1) have large eyes and feed by making short sprints ended with a peck, enabling them to reach small crustaceans and worms (4) on which they feed. Redshanks (2) also hunt by sight, and have medium-length bills with which they can probe the mud and reach small invertebrates and worms (4, 5). Curlews (3) use their long curved bill to reach deep into sand and mud to extract molluscs (6), lugworms and ragworms (7).

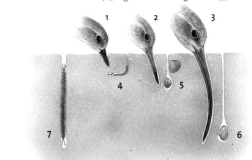

Oystercatcher (*Haematopus ostralegus*) Large wader with distinctive bold black-and-white plumage and bright orange bill. Resident in Britain, and also a passage migrant and winter visitor. Nests on the ground. Feeds on cockles and mussels, which it opens by hammering and prising with its bill.

Sanderling (*Calidris alba*) Breeds further north than Britain, where it is a passage migrant and winter visitor confined to coasts. Runs along the water's edge in a characteristic fashion, in and out among the waves, picking up small molluscs, worms and shrimps.

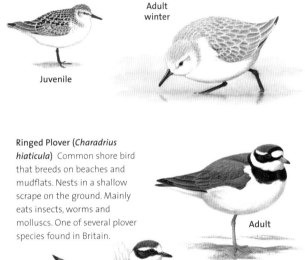

Adult winter

Juvenile

Ringed Plover (*Charadrius hiaticula*) Common shore bird that breeds on beaches and mudflats. Nests in a shallow scrape on the ground. Mainly eats insects, worms and molluscs. One of several plover species found in Britain.

Adult

Juvenile

Dunlin (*Calidris alpina*)
Summer visitor or resident
occurring on seashores,
mudflats, creeks and
estuaries, as well as visiting
inland waters. Nests in a
grassy cup well hidden on
the ground. Feeds on small
invertebrates such as
molluscs and worms.

Juvenile

Adult
summer

Adult
winter

Redshank (*Tringa totanus*) Grey-
brown wader with a characteristic
red bill and legs. Winters on coasts,
especially in estuaries and on
mudflats. Breeds both near coasts
and inland. Feeds principally
on invertebrates.

Juvenile

Adult
breeding

Curlew (*Numenius arquata*) Largest wader, with a very long decurved bill. Resident in Britain. Breeds on wet meadows and moors; winters on coasts. Eats mainly small invertebrates, fishes and plant matter.

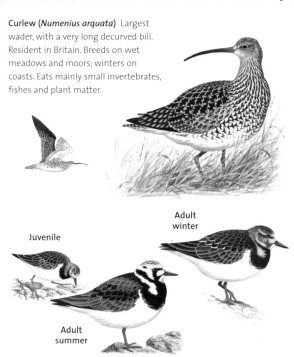

Adult winter

Juvenile

Adult summer

Turnstone (*Arenaria interpres*) Boldly marked wader that breeds along coasts and stony tundra. Winters on rocky coasts and breakwaters from Britain to the Mediterranean. Diet is mainly insects, molluscs and crustaceans, which it finds by using its bill to overturn pebbles and pieces of algae.

Black-headed Gull (*Chroicocephalus ridibundus*)

Common on coasts in winter, and in other locations, across northern Europe. Breeds in colonies. Feeds on invertebrates and seeds, as well as scavenging in rubbish.

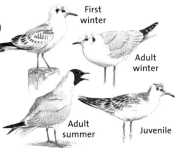

First winter

Adult winter

Adult summer

Juvenile

Adult

Juvenile

Second winter

Herring Gull (*Larus argentatus*)

Abundant on coast, and common inland in winter. Nest a bulky mound of flotsam and grass. Diet includes fishes, crustaceans, carrion and birds. Similar Common Gull (*L. canus*) is smaller and has yellow-green legs.

Lesser Black-backed Gull (*Larus fuscus*)

Found on coasts and sea; may breed on inland fresh waters. Eats almost anything, including fishes, small mammals, birds and their eggs, and carrion. Greater Black-backed Gull (*L. marinus*) is much larger, with similar plumage colours.

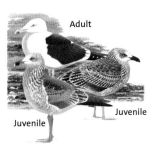

Adult

Juvenile

Juvenile

Sandwich Tern (*Sterna sandvicensis*) Britain's largest tern. Breeds in enormous colonies in shingle and sand coastal locations in northern Europe, wintering further south. Eats fishes and other marine invertebrates.

Adult winter

Adult summer

Juvenile

Adult winter

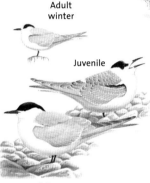

Juvenile

Common Tern (*Sterna hirundo*) A summer visitor to Britain that comes to breed on shingle beaches and rocky islands. Like all terns, it flies gracefully and feeds on fishes.

Adult summer

Adult winter

Arctic Tern (*Sterna paradisaea*) Breeds in colonies along northern European coasts, nesting in a shallow scrape in sand or grass. Winters in the south. Feeds on fishes, crustaceans, molluscs and insects.

Adult summer

Eurasian Otter
Lutra lutra

SIZE AND DESCRIPTION Length to 84cm (body); 48cm
(tail). A streamlined carnivore of the mustelid family
whose body is adapted to an aquatic lifestyle. Water-resistant fur is
dense, consisting of short hairs and longer paler guard hairs. Feet are
webbed, and tail is long and powerful. Upperparts are dark brown,
chin and upper throat paler, and underparts markedly paler.
HABITAT AND ECOLOGY Found in coastal areas and wetlands, and in rivers.
Normally active by night. Nests in a burrow (holt). Diet includes fishes,
other small vertebrates and crustaceans.
DISTRIBUTION Once found throughout Europe, but became extinct in
many areas. Now protected and expanding in Britain.

Common Seal
Phoca vitulina

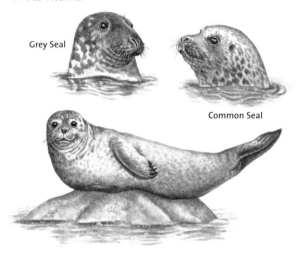

Grey Seal

Common Seal

SIZE AND DESCRIPTION Length 1.2–1.6m. Small seal with a short muzzle and V-shaped nostrils. Colour variable, but usually greyish with darker mottling, and white whiskers. Britain is also home to a major part of the global population of the larger (to 3.3m long) Grey Seal (*Halichoerus grypus*), which has a characteristic 'Roman' nose.

HABITAT AND ECOLOGY Typically found in sandflats and estuaries, as well as on rocky shores in Scotland. Single pup is born each year on a beach or sandbar; it is active and swims in the sea from birth. Seals hunt for fishes underwater, and also feed on shellfish and crustaceans.

DISTRIBUTION Both Common and Grey Seals breed on northern European coasts, including British and Irish shores.

Index